"Lead like a girl! This book is a call to arms, an enthusiastic, exciting, insightful manifesto for anyone who knows she can make a difference."

Seth Godin
Author
The Icarus Deception, Tribes, Poke the Box and The Purple Cow

WONDER WOMEN:

HOW WESTERN WOMEN
WILL SAVE THE WORLD

By
Jessica Eaves Mathews
& Phil Dyer

To Wonder Women Everywhere.

ωW

WONDER WOMEN:

HOW WESTERN WOMEN
WILL SAVE THE WORLD

By
Jessica Eaves Mathews
& Phil Dyer

WONDER WOMEN:
HOW WESTERN WOMEN WILL SAVE THE WORLD

TABLE OF CONTENTS

THE BROKEN AMERICAN DREAM

OUR SALVATION: WHO WE ARE IS WHAT WE NEED

HOW WESTERN WOMEN WILL SAVE THE WORLD

ACKNOWLEDGMENTS

We aren't big believers in coincidence or "happy accidents"… some things are just meant to be. When we met in a high-level business mastermind in early 2010, we immediately clicked and knew – almost from Day 1 – that we'd be doing a BIG project together. There've been some twists and turns along the way, including a title change (or two), starting a total of 5 (and counting) new ventures between the two of us, and dealing with all of the other distractions the Universe tends to throw at you when you're on the cusp of a major breakthrough.

Through it all, we stayed positive, supported each other through the challenges, and stayed connected with our "WHY" for this book, which is truly a call to action for forward-thinking women (and men) to reject the "I win by you losing" business model and embrace the power and possibilities of collaborative success. Our authentic hope is that this book can act as a catalyst and thought-changer to transform how we – as a society and as business owners – view success.

THANKS FROM JESSICA AND PHIL

While the concepts and ideas contained in this book represent our decades of combined business, professional, and leadership experience, we've also drawn heavily on work of other brilliant authors, entrepreneurs, business owners, and thought leaders. We would be remiss in not recognizing the amazing work of a number of trailblazers and have endeavored to give them credit at every possible turn.

They include – but aren't limited to – Seth Godin, Arianna Huffington, Dan Pink, Sara Blakely, Sir Ken Robinson, Jessica Jackley, Sir Richard Branson, and many, many others.

In addition, no book like this comes together without MANY hours of support from the editors, designers, graphic artists, and assistants that helped us every step of the way. In particular, we want to thank the incredible Sara Blette and her incredible team who jumped in to rescue us very late in the game, creating a beautiful piece of work while still enabling us to meet a ridiculously tight publication deadline. We are humbled and very thankful for all of your creative and hard work.

We'd also like to thank photographer Norman Watkins for his great publicity photography.

Finally, we want to thank all of the incredible entrepreneurs and thought leaders who gave so generously of their time and energy during the interviews we conducted while crafting this book. You'll see many of them throughout the book and more to come at our website, www.wonderwomenbook.com.

SPECIAL THANKS FROM JESSICA

If I listed everyone that I'd like to extend special thanks to, it would fill another book! First, I want to recognize my mom and dad - Mel and Mary Ann Eaves - for their unwavering support and the many sacrifices they have made to help me reach my dreams and sticking with me even when they couldn't exactly figure out what I was doing. Also, I want to thank my little girl Kate, who's quickly developing into an amazing young woman (and future Wonder Woman) and is my daily inspiration and the reason I get out of bed and do what I do everyday. Kate, your unconditional love, patience and total belief in me have helped make this book possible.

I'd also want to thank all of the wonderful business mentors, confidants, and mastermind partners who've provided timely insight, guidance, and, when needed, a big dose of reality. In particular, I want to thank my dear friends and mastermind buddies Lisa Manyon, Jennifer Longmore, and Angela Jia Kim for your friendship, wisdom, brilliance, humor and strength – each of you have helped me know what is possible for me and have kept the faith year in and year out. Finally, I'd like to thank my co-author and fellow traveler on this fantastic journey, Phil Dyer. You are absolutely brilliant and have been such an invaluable support, kick in the pants and friend throughout the journey of the past three years. I'm grateful to have you in my corner! It's been an awesome and inspiring ride so far and it's just beginning!

PERSONAL THANKS FROM PHIL DYER

I'm extraordinarily thankful to those who've selflessly supported me throughout this sometimes trying process of late nights, early mornings, and tight deadlines. In particular, my wife Kerry and great kids Alexander and Lilly, who always seemed to be there at the right time with a hug or word of encouragement.

I've been inspired from an early age by my mother, Marilyn Dyer Blair, whose entrepreneurial courage in the face of incredible adversity provided me a clear vision of what's possible through business ownership. I'd also like to recognize two other incredible entrepreneurs who never fail to challenge and support me, Larry Broughton and Angelique Rewers.

Last – and certainly not least – I want to thank Jessica Eaves Mathews – whose intellect, energy, patience, and friendship never cease to amaze me. Thank you so much for everything you do…you are truly a force of nature!

When morality comes up against profit, it is seldom that profit loses.

– Shirley Chisholm

INTRODUCTION

Let's play a word association game...

If we say Enron, MCI WorldCom, BP, Lehman Brothers, Bernie Madoff, banking crisis, mortgage mess, fiscal cliff...where do your thoughts go? What images do these words elicit in your mind's eye?

Do you picture corrupt, greedy CEOs?

Do you think of success at any cost, no matter the social cost or who gets stepped on? Do you imagine clueless politicians who argue endlessly and are far more focused on "winning" than on doing what is right? Do you see the uncaring bureaucrat whose blind adherence to idiotic rules made it virtually impossible to start (or grow) your small business?

Perhaps you have been personally impacted by those above – or people just like them. Maybe you have lost your job, your home, or the financial stability you toiled for years building up through your investments in your house or retirement account. No matter how you have witnessed or experienced the events in the corporate, small business and political America over the past three to five years, there's one inescapable conclusion. America's business model is irretrievably broken.

For the past 125-plus years, the American dream of wealth and business ownership has been achieved through a male-dominated "I win by you losing" and "I must win at all costs" mindset. This "ends justify the means as long as I come out on top" approach gradually made it acceptable for people to compromise their ethics, blindly pursue their vision of success regardless of the collateral damage, and eventually sacrifice their very humanity on the altar of excess and greed. This slow erosion of our collective consciousness became a destructive cancer that resulted in the near collapse of our entire economy. It is a testosterone-driven, cutthroat business environment that prevents sustainable prosperity, destroys any semblance of the healthy work-life balance, and eventually destroys jobs, entrepreneurial opportunity and entire communities. While these attitudes originated on Wall Street and in the halls of Congress, the myriad of challenges they have spawned have become very real – and devastating – Main Street problems.

Remember Gordon Gecko? He taught us that "Greed is Good."

And think back on the famous line from the Godfather, or the tag line for the Apprentice: "It's Not Personal. It's Just Business."

Have you ever really thought about that quote? What does that mean, really? Do you really want to live in a society where all humanity is removed from business? For those of us who are striving to align our business pursuits with who we are on an authentic level, the idea of segregating what is "personal" or "human" from "business" seems unnatural and is a recipe for…well…the very kind of disaster we have just experienced as a country and as an economy.

Through this disaster, we should have learned that capitalism without a conscience is dangerous. We should have also learned that the kind of people who thrive and get ahead in that kind of society will always focus on getting as much as they can for as long as they can, regardless of the consequences to anyone else.

Stop for a moment and ask yourself out loud, "How does the economic and financial turmoil of the last few years make me feel?"

Just sit with that for a moment or two...pretty depressing stuff, isn't it?

Well...that's the bad news and we are going to kick that to the curb! It is time to take our country back! It is time to inject our business dealings with humanity – to make it personal, once again. It is time to value collaboration, connection and community over the ego. We may not be able to directly control what is currently happening with Wall Street or Congress, but we can certainly take back Main Street.

The good news is there's a massive, seismic shift occurring in the business world. Like the inexorable swing of a giant pendulum, this force is clearing the way towards a more sustainable, more socially responsible and even human-minded business model. This transformational movement harnesses the collaborative and cooperative power of feminine energy and will completely reshape the way America does business. For those who choose to embrace it, this shift will create an unstoppable tsunami of economic opportunity and self-sufficiency that will literally change the world!

Now, don't get us wrong...

We aren't going to spend time in this book bashing men or the "typical" male traits. We like men and Phil happens to be one! We both think the male energy and approach to life and business is enormously valuable and a necessary part of a balanced approach to life and business. That said, the unhealthy emphasis and downright worship of the grotesquely exaggerated "hyper-male" traits found in the Machiavellian approach to business has cost us dearly. This must change if we hope to emerge from the economic hole that we've dug ourselves into. In short, we believe that it's time to save the world!

Further, we believe that you – the current (or aspiring) female business owner, entrepreneur and business leader – are uniquely positioned to become a new

Western Women

WILL save the world

if WE CAN EMBRACE the POWER of

collaboration

FOCUS on responsible

BUSINESS PRACTICES

and allow ourselves to BALANCE

results-driven MALE ENERGY

with the intuitive

FEMALE consciousness

and empathy TOWARDS OTHERS.

breed of business super hero. With the hyper-male model failing badly, we must step forward and demonstrate a new kind of leadership within our businesses and communities, one woman and one business owner at a time – whether we have one employee or a thousand. We must blaze a new trail going forward – one that's marked with success instead of excess, significance instead of selfishness, compassion instead of corruption, and empathy instead of apathy.

We must embrace the power and possibilities of the feminine energy to create a new business compact with our team members, our customers and ourselves. We must build our business structures that take care of all those who are participating in or affected by our business operations – our employees, clients, customers, communities, and yes, even ourselves.

We aren't the only ones who recognize this coming tsunami. The **Dalai Lama**, speaking at the Peace Summit in Vancouver in 2009, predicted that **"Western women will save the world."**

Stop for a moment and consider the positive impact this can create for our clients and customers, our team members, our communities, and ultimately ourselves. North American businesswomen like yourselves (yes, Canadian sisters, we are also talking about you!) are uniquely situated to lead this revolution because you have the education, the freedom, the experience (thank Rosie the Riveter for that!) and now the vision to be catalysts of change that our business model so desperately needs.

This book is both a call to action and a guide for a radical shift in the way we do business—a better business, a better life, a better world. If you are willing to put on your cape, your big girl panties and strike your best super hero pose, then it all starts with YOU!

Are you ready to fly? Then let's go...

– *Jessica Eaves Mathews & Phil Dyer*

THE BROKEN
AMERICAN DREAM

Yes, the American Dream is broken. Sort of. But don't worry. We aren't going to bash America here. We love America. We are blessed to live in the best country on earth (okay, places like Canada and Australia are pretty great too!). Our purpose in this section is to **look with a critical and honest eye at our business model in the western part of the world and diagnose why we have come to a point of crisis economically and ethically.** Just bear with us in the next few chapters, because things might seem a bit bleak as you read them. We promise that after we turn over some big rocks and look at the truth, we will give you the solution. **There is hope and plenty of it.** So keep that in mind as you read on, and we will see you on the other side.

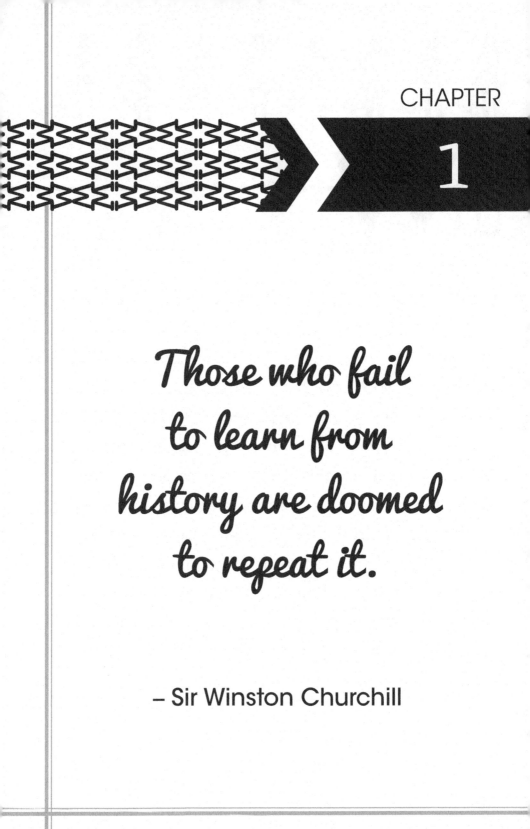

*Those who fail
to learn from
history are doomed
to repeat it.*

– Sir Winston Churchill

We Need a Hero(ine)

Can you remember the last time we had a strong business leader in this country?

Someone who stood on principle and inspired people to be better, live better and truly make a difference instead of just making piles of money? Someone who continuously looked beyond the bottom line and remained committed to not only what was good for his or her company and shareholders, but to what was good for his or her customers, team members, suppliers, and broader community?

Unfortunately, there are precious few in recent years who we can use as role models for building a business in which the leaders think beyond the next quarter's results and how those results will impact their stock options.

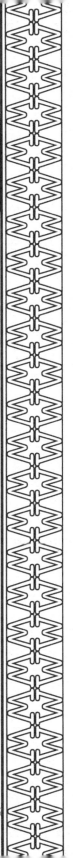

We have virtually no role models in Corporate America who have shown us how to successfully integrate spirituality, emotion, and intellect with a thriving business. Instead, we've been treated to a sickening parade of corruption and greed from those who have risen to the top of the business world to then only to use their positions solely for their own financial gain.

Over the last decade, the dishonesty and callousness of these so-called business "leaders" towards their employees, shareholders and customers has grown increasingly shocking. We've seen Ken Lay, the CEO of Enron, drive his organization, shareholders, and employees into bankruptcy. We've seen Bernie Ebbers, CEO of WorldCom, engage in a fraud and conspiracy that cost his investors $100 billion and ruined countless lives. We've seen Bernie Madoff, founder and chairman of Bernard L. Madoff Investment Securities, admit that his investment firm was merely a complex ponzi scheme, the largest investor fraud ever perpetrated by an individual. And most recently, we've seen Jon Corzine of MF Global steal over a billion dollars from customer accounts to cover trading losses, with virtually no accountability or repercussions because of his political connections. All of this financial devastation was caused by profound financial greed. The "I must win at all costs" mindset invariably means that countless others will lose.

Those four examples reflect organizations built on a house of cards, with those at the top enjoying the fruits of their ascension, while being wilfully blind to the consequences of their actions. The people who invested in and worked for those companies were betrayed and left holding an empty bag by those they had trusted to protect their futures. And this trend isn't a recent one or just a product of our new millennium—in every decade, you can see business leaders who built empires out of greed and self-service. And when those empires were subjected to public inspection, they collapsed, resulting nationwide panic and harm.

So, how did we get here? An examination of the past 100-125 years shows two main sources of the problem we now face:

(1) Our class system;

(2) Our educational system.

Shirley Chisholm, the first black woman elected to Congress and a vocal advocate for healthcare and social services reform, once said, "When morality comes up against profit, it is seldom that profit loses." This has been the case in America for centuries now—a nation that was founded on freedom and potential quickly stratified into upper and lower classes, robber barons and factory workers, socialites and servants (although not with the rigid social caste system of most other countries).

How exactly did this separation happen, and how did the cultural divide result in the slow corruption of big business? As explained under Don Beck's Spiral Dynamics theory, America's business practices are reflections of its cultural values. That is, the American people as a whole have collectively gone through certain developmental stages as to values and those values can be seen illustrated in our business practices and norms.

For example, in the 1750s, America was struggling for independence and so it was a time to be strategic and aggressively fight for our freedom and our own beliefs as a new country. What got us through this time was a strong masculine energy and it was because of that focus, intensity, aggression and unwavering determination that we found our own place in the world and freedom from the rule of the English monarchy. It was this strong focus on personal success and independence that eventually transposed itself onto American business practices—and thus business became a self-centered affair.

Because our country was based on freedom of livelihood and expression (at least for the wealthy, white men), business evolved with a similar mindset. It was about creating independent wealth, owning property, and having power and influence over your community and nation. During this time, America came to be seen as "the land of opportunity," where your social status (or lack thereof) didn't necessarily determine where you actually went in life. The abundant "rags to riches" stories emanating from our shores drew immigrants in droves, all seeking a better life.

We continued to need this type of energy and focus as we became an established country and solid government, which continued even through the American Civil War in the mid 1800s. It was the acceleration of the Industrial Revolution in the United States in the late 1800s and early 1900s that really sent this mentality into overdrive.

As we emerged as a world leader and innovator in politics, business and technology, the focus turned to who could make the most money the fastest? Who could corner the market and accumulate the most material possessions, influence and power? While this drive for innovation and power is the heart of the entrepreneurial spirit, it also led to a male-dominated, competitive marketplace entirely focused on the bottom line, rather than focusing also on the impact of business activities on the people affected and served by them.

In fact, in order to function and keep our economy going, we needed armies of workers for the assembly lines in our factories – and legions of semi-skilled immigrants fit the bill perfectly. As a result, our educational system was developed to create these "worker bees," with the most valuable students being the ones who followed directions, not those who challenged authority and questioned their role in the system. Those worker bees unknowingly kept the system going, but did not benefit greatly from it except by being given the illusion of job security. (As we saw during the Great Depression and again in the most recent Great Recession of 2007–09 (and counting), job stability has turned out to be nothing more than a myth and a carrot to keep the worker bees working. But we digress…)

WOMEN IN THE INDUSTRIAL ECONOMY

In the United States and Canada, women at least got the opportunity for an education in this system, unlike girls and women in many other places around the world. However, education did not provide many opportunities for women even as our country grew in stature. Until well into the 1900s, women had no right to vote in the US, Canada or even the UK. They had few legal rights, and were often forced to marry in order to achieve status or financial security. There were very few ways in which they could participate in the accumulation of wealth and independence. In fact, virtually no one could, except elite, white males.

Certainly, there were a few notable exceptions, such as Sarah Breedlove Walker, better known as Madam C.J. Walker (b. 1867 – d. 1919) who became America's first self-made female millionaire. She created her fortune by creating, manufacturing, and selling beauty and hair products specifically designed for fellow black women. Walker and those like her were a fortunate few who broke free of class and economic limitations and created the extraordinary out of nothing, but their ability to do so was not learned or encouraged in school or in the workplace. Everyone else played a willing (or unwilling) supporting role in the development of our ever-growing economic power.

It was during World War II that women got their first real taste of financial independence as they went to work in the factories making munitions and war supplies place of our men who were away fighting the war. The famous icon for what turned out to be a massive turning point in our culture was Rosie the Riveter. At the time, women largely saw it as their patriotic duty to fill in for the men and support the war effort. But for many women, working outside the home changed everything and launched the beginning of what we know today as the feminist movement.

Women discovered that they liked making money and liked learning a trade. So when the men came home from the war, many women refused to stop working. They began to desire the same work and financial opportunities that were available to men.

However, it wasn't until the 1960s and 70s when the feminist movement came to full tilt. At that time, women demanded to be treated equally to men in all respects, and there was a belief that in order for women to succeed in business, they basically had to become like men. A great movie that illustrates the struggle that many women experienced is *Baby Boom* with Diane Keaton. That movie shows us a glimpse into the 1980s corporate world where if you were a woman, you had to behave like a man (even though men had had the added luxury of having wives at home making their lives possible at the office). In that world, if you wanted balance, children or any kind of a life outside of the boardroom, you were immediately marginalized and pushed aside.

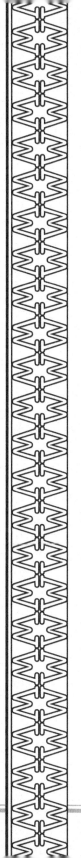

Sadly, that mentality has created an unhealthy environment in Corporate America, leaving many companies focused on the bottom line to the exclusion of family, the environment, employees and even ethics. Despite some positive changes (and a lot more lip service and platitudes) over the last two decades, this is still the state of Corporate America today. We seem to be "stuck on stupid" and either unwilling or unable to move past the attitudes that contributed to the near collapse of our economy and produced such miscreants as Ken Lay and Bernie Maddoff.

A NEW DAY DAWNS

Now that we are over a decade into the new millennium, however, the pendulum has begun to swing the other way. The nearly unbroken string of excesses, scandals and bursting bubbles we've seen since 2000 have made it painfully clear that we can no longer ignore the mess the unbalanced, hyper-male approach in business has created for all of us. We've been sequentially whipsawed by: the Tech Bubble (Dot-Com Bomb), the Housing Bubble, the Banking Crisis, and now pervasive and persistent unemployment/underemployment. Those that are paying attention are recognizing that things must change radically in order to save our economy and our future. In addition, many women are slowly coming to the very simple, yet profoundly powerful realization...they don't have to act like a man in order to get ahead! And what is more important, they don't want to act like a man any longer!

Millions of working women, especially in Corporate America, have spent their entire careers leaving a big part of whom they are at the door in order to fit in and get ahead. The result?

Women spend up to 80% of each day putting on a persona that isn't totally authentic – a persona that leaves out vital personality traits, values and priorities. Women are increasingly depressed and dissatisfied in Corporate America and are leaving it behind to create businesses that reflect who they are at their core.

Thankfully, this quest for relief and a way to earn a living without compromising who we are any longer turns out to be the exact solution for our salvation economically. This is what the Dalai Lama recognized in late 2009 when he stated that it would be Western Women who would save the world.

So what does this mean for you? It means that after centuries of aggression in a male-dominated marketplace, businesses on Main Street are quietly moving away from the single-minded "profit above all else" focus towards a more balanced, community-minded, collaborative mindset.

Another reason for the move away from self-centered, male-dominated approach to business is that many successful business people, after having reached the top, are starting to long for meaning—searching for significance beyond a corner office, reserved parking spot, a McMansion, and big bank account. Increasing numbers of people are no longer content with stoically plodding along in jobs they hate for 30–40 years, bereft of happiness, towards the mythical promised land of retirement. We are now starting to seek fulfilment along with a paycheck.

This wave of cultural change is a direct result of the rising tide of feminine energy. It is starting to bring balance back to business and to our society as a whole. It's the balance of the feminine and masculine energies in business that create the cornerstone for how Western Women will become the modern day superheroes. In order to compete in our new global economy, a business must bring its humanity into the office and the boardroom in order to better connect with clients and customers, and it must efficiently use technology to do so. Those who ignore the signs of this global business tsunami do so at their extreme peril. We firmly believe that those who fail to catch the "front edge" of this powerful, transformative wave will eventually be washed away and left behind – essentially becoming "business flotsam." Don't let this happen to you!

Now, let us pause for a moment to address what some of you may be thinking. We are not talking about Socialism here and we're both unapologetic capitalists! We are talking about business owners who want to make a profit - a healthy profit. Just like you, we want financial security for ourselves and our families.

But beyond a need for profitable security, a big part of the shift we are describing is about balancing the pursuit of profit with the needs of our families, our friends, our team members, our communities and ultimately, the planet. This movement is now picking up steam and experiencing rapid growth through "new" mediums like the Internet and social media.

People now have the ability to instantly connect, share a message, and even create a following with millions of diverse people from across the globe through Facebook, LinkedIn, Twitter, Pinterest, YouTube, and personal blogs. We are connected and communicating, which sets the stage for the rise of the more cooperative, feminine energy in business dealings.

Rather than the old-school, male business model of success – typified by black suits, briefcases, jealously-guarded business secrets, an unhealthy focus on competitors (instead of clients and customers) and cookie-cutter careers – this new, balanced, community-minded, collaborative energy embraces and celebrates people's unique gifts and skills and, as a result, has begun opening up multiple paths to success.

HOLY DOLLAR SIGNS, WONDER WOMAN!

Creating a community and globally conscious business that is balanced in how it approaches its people and its profits will allow you to ride the wave rather than be swept under by it.

The male-centric mindset, which holds that only a few can succeed at the expense of many, still dominates much of Corporate America (despite the frequent financial and emotional ruin it's wrought over the last few decades), but the façade is beginning to crack and that crack is now too big to repair! More and more people in the business world – both women and men – can sense the shift and feel that changes are coming, but they aren't sure what it is and how it will effect them. They understand that the current business model is irretrievably broken and are searching for leader who can show them a new path and take them in a different direction.

They're yearning for the benefits of what Seth Godin, a progressive American entrepreneur and author, has called a tribe—that is, being surrounded by people who support you and encourage you, who give you good ideas and constructive criticism but still hold you accountable for your actions. The marketplace is moving away from a cutthroat business ideal and toward a collaborative, cooperative environment. We must surround ourselves with people who not only make us shine entrepreneurially, but who tell us when we go too far and forget ourselves in greed, ambition or abdication of personal responsibility.

We believe it is imperative to merge these two powerful forces – balancing feminine compassion with masculine aggression – to form a new business model for a new world. We must stop being distracted by shiny fads and dazzling marketing campaigns and get back to the heart of what businesses really are at their core: Organizations that are not just about the bottom line, but that are created by human beings in order to serve, to fulfill, to improve and to innovate.

"A BUSINESS THAT MAKES NOTHING BUT MONEY IS POOR BUSINESS."

– Henry Ford

You must bring your whole, integrated self into YOUR BUSINESS CARRYING YOUR humanity with your business savvy through the office door.

Of course, many would scoff at this—as Donald Trump has famously said, "It's not personal. It's business." Well, we're here to say that's bunk…it IS personal at a very deep and visceral level! You must bring your whole, integrated self into your business, carrying your humanity with your business savvy through the office door. There is nothing wrong with desiring wealth, financial independence and even luxury. We are capitalists first and foremost and both of us pursue our businesses with the intent of maximizing profits. However, we believe in a capitalistic economy you can achieve this level of success without other people having to lose in the process. You can offer a product or service that benefits society, that is sold through a company that respects and values its team members, clients and customers, its community and still make money!

So, how do you do that? You start by donning your cape and becoming one of the Wonder Women, who are making the business streets safe again for all of us. This new generation of business superheroes makes up a growing movement of people who refuse to check their conscience at the door to make a profit and who care about significance and positive impact just as much (if not more) than they do about success.

Wonder Women buy into the wisdom of the late Zig Ziglar whole-heartedly,

"YOU WILL GET ALL YOU WANT OUT OF LIFE, IF YOU HELP ENOUGH OTHER PEOPLE GET WHAT THEY WANT."

– Zig Ziglar

Meet the New
SUPER HEROES*!*

So who are some of these Wonder Women we keep referring to? We are thrilled to introduce you to a few stand outs.

JESSICA JACKLEY, Kiva.org and Profounder

One of the most inspiring young entrepreneurs who exemplify this movement is Jessica Jackley, the co-founder and CEO of Kiva.org, the first person-to-person micro-lending site. After traveling to Africa and getting to know local villagers, and seeing both their work ethic and the importance of their small businesses to the local economy, Jessica realized that even a small loan could change their lives and homes forever. With her partner, Matt Flannery, she set up Kiva, which cuts through the red-tape of banking institutions to allow individuals to loan as little as $25 to businesses in third-world and developing countries. Now, Kiva has donated over $200 million dollars to entrepreneurs in 220 countries. Kiva.org is a great example of conscious capitalism—Jessica has extremely successful companies, but does so with heart and accountability.

RICHARD BRANSON, BLAKE MYCOSKIE, TONY HSIEH

Of course, our list of super heroes doesn't just include women and no list would be complete without mentioning high-profile entrepreneurs like Richard Branson, billionaire owner of Virgin Group, Blake Mycoskie, founder of Toms Shoes, and Tony Hsieh, founder of Zappos.com, all of whom took chances with business ventures and allowed both themselves and their team members to work outside of the box. Tony Hsieh in particular focused on extreme customer service and satisfaction and as a result created a cult-like following of customers and eventually sold his company to Amazon.com for over $900 million dollars—just from selling shoes online. And all three have succeeded at both making their worlds and the people in them better while turning a generous profit.

Real change is going to start in the trenches, with small business owners and entrepreneurs like you.

ANGELA JIA KIM, Om Aroma + Co, Savor Spa, Savor The Success

Another recent business star is Angela Jia Kim, who started as a renowned classical pianist and went on to found her own organic skincare line, Om Aroma, which has now won numerous accolades and garnered a celebrity following. But it's not just another addition to the beauty field that makes her notable—it's also the way she sells her skincare line. Angela has instituted a "Dollars and Scents" program that hires women who are re-transitioning into the workplace after taking time off to raise children. Mothers who take time off are often marginalized, and, if they are homemakers for too many years, are seen as valueless in the workplace—what could they possibly have to offer? But Angela recognizes that being a mother is a great skill in and of itself, one requires multitasking, organizing, and peacemaking, all necessities in the modern workplace. So, she is empowering women while also making a profit: another example of conscious capitalism.

She is also committed to giving a portion of all proceeds for the sale of her skincare products to charities chosen by her customers. As she says, "Let's make the world more beautiful together! Good for the skin. Good for the world." As if that wasn't enough, Angela has also found a powerful way to use her lessons-learned in business to help empower other women entrepreneurs through her second company, Savor the Success, which provides leadership, information, community, support and encouragement for a network of over 20,000 members across the US and Canada.

www.savorthesuccess.com
www.omaroma.com

You will hear more about Jessica and Angela later in the book.

Inspiring right? Okay, we have to admit that this kind of balanced, humanitarian-based approach to business isn't the norm yet. It is still in its early stages and will require some courage to pursue. Before this new mindset becomes mainstream, people may look at you like you're crazy when you say that you're going to focus on being happy and feeling fulfilled, and on making sure your clients are happy and fulfilled, rather than just on buying a fancy new car or a bigger house. They may laugh at you and try to talk you out of it—but just because they're not ready to take that step doesn't mean you shouldn't.

NOTES

If you are always trying to be normal, you will never know how amazing you can be.

– Maya Angelou

America's Educational System: The Anti-Creativity Factory

12-hour days. Joyless, gray-walled cubicles. Mind-numbing repetitive tasks day after day. Un-engaged. Un-enthused. No visibility on the impact and/or significance of your efforts.

Welcome to the 40-year plus purgatory that many women in corporate America find themselves trapped in. They desperately cling to outmoded societal definitions of "success" in the workplace and toil away, lurching towards the hazy beacon of retirement that flickers in the distance. Sounds appealing, doesn't it?

Collectively, many women have bought into (or have been sold) the idea that "success" means a nice house in a nice neighborhood, a nice car, a nice vacation once a year, a nice private school education for the kids, and money in the bank for retirement. They just blindly accept that to achieve "success," they've got to show up every day, check a big piece of who they are at the door each morning, conform to the culture of their employer's organization, labor away without complaint, and then rinse and repeat.

A recent survey by the Gallup organization revealed a frightening statistic:

An astounding 70% percent of employees are either "NOT ENGAGED" or "ACTIVELY DISENGAGED" on the job.

With that level of disengagement, it's a wonder anyhing happens in most organizations!

http://www.gallup.com/content/162953/tackle-employees-stagnating-engagement.aspv

Women avoid making waves or standing out, preferring to perform their jobs to the minimum standard needed to get good reviews, an annual raise and – if they're lucky – a small bonus.

Unfortunately, while conforming their lives to fit this approved blueprint to "happiness," millions of women in this country are actually living quiet lives of desperation. What is so sad is that despite their dissatisfaction, they just accept that this is just the way it is. They blindly follow "the rules" and don't even question them.

They just accept this as the way life is and they all march along in lockstep trusting that the system works. You might not think of yourself as a follower, but very few people actually think outside the "box" or even fewer actually live outside the "box" that society has set up. For many, even the thought of living outside the box paralyzes them with fear. And that's exactly how the powers-that-be have designed, promoted, reinforced, and perpetuated the system to their benefit for decades.

The "RULES"
of conformity

o **Work hard**

o **Keep your head down**

o **Don't complain or draw attention to yourself**

o **Dutifully save for retirement someday**

o **In retirement, you'll finally be allowed to pursue your heart's desires**

How did we end up as a society of virtual automatons who - for the most part - blindly and blithely live our lives as we're are told to do, even though the experience is demoralizing, discouraging and often painful for so many?

Think about it. When you ask a 5-year-old what she wants to be when she grows up, there are infinite answers. Most likely, the answers center on an activity that she loves. She might want to be a ballerina, a movie star, a veterinarian, a zookeeper, a horse trainer or even an astronaut (because it means flying to the stars). She might want to be a famous painter, or writer, or musician. If you ask that same child five years later, when she's ten, the answers will most likely be reduced to about ten "socially accepted" answers. By this point, she'll tell you she wants to be a doctor, or a lawyer, or teacher or nurse. Now on the surface, there's nothing wrong with that, since these are all important professions that society needs.

However, it makes you wonder: What happens in that five year period that smooshed her dreams, imagination, and limitless possibilities into a handful of approved "respectable" pursuits?

The answer might surprise you. The source of the problem is actually rooted in the educational system in the United States.

Today's educational system was created primarily during the Industrial Revolution and is essentially intended as a breeding hive for factory worker bees. At the time, our economic system was dependent heavily upon the steady output of factories, which were in turn wholly dependent upon an army of subservient, obedient, reliable factory workers. Without them, the system would fail. So, our educational system was designed to create generations of worker bees to fill this demand for years to come.

These students were taught from day one in the school system that the qualities valued most were: achieving perfect attendance, being punctual, being good at rote memorization, having respect for authority, speaking only when spoken to, and being a "good" girl, which involved sitting quietly with her hands folded on your lap and making her teacher's life as easy as possible by following all directions without questioning or challenging them. Kids who questioned, challenged or had a hard time fitting into this system were labeled as problems, delinquent and were either prevented from getting ahead or shuffled off to "alternative" schools.

Those who displayed the desired qualities of conformity were rewarded with good grades and eventually the sought after jobs in the factories. Thinking independently or being a creative problem solver was not valued and was actively discouraged.

Unfortunately, even as we moved past the Industrial Age, are on the tail end of the Information/Technology Age, and are rapidly entering the Relationship Age, we're still educating our youth to fit into the factory-worker mentality. Is it any wonder that we're slipping in innovation and – consequently economic strength – as a country?

EVERYBODY IS A GENIUS,
BUT IF YOU JUDGE
A FISH BY ITS ABILITY
TO CLIMB A TREE,
IT WILL LIVE ITS
WHOLE LIFE BELIEVING
THAT IT IS STUPID.

- Albert Einstein

New York Times best selling author Seth Godin and all-around smart guy asks, "As we get ready for the 93rd year of universal public education, here's the question every parent and taxpayer needs to wrestle with: Are we going to applaud, push or even permit our schools (including most of the private ones) to continue the safe but ultimately doomed strategy of churning out predictable, testable and mediocre factory-workers?" He concludes, "As long as we embrace (or even accept) standardized testing, fear of science, little attempt at teaching leadership and most of all, the bureaucratic imperative to turn education into a factory itself, we're in big trouble."

The challenge posed by today's dynamic business environment is that far too many people become mentally paralyzed when called upon to think outside the box. As a result, many organizations lumber about like giant dinosaurs, handicapped by an antiquated, top down, command-and-control management system that might be great for producing widgets (or Model Ts), but is dreadfully inadequate to deal with ever-shifting market conditions and rapidly evolving technology. According to far too many managers, if it isn't in the employee handbook, doesn't have a proven track record, or isn't a "safe play," it doesn't exist or is flat-out wrong.

> Most workers quickly learn that standing out from the pack makes them a target for managers who prefer blind obedience and loyalty and soon blend into the anonymity and safety of the herd.

Workers are rewarded for being diligent, as opposed to being effective. Experiments and failures are frowned up and rewarded with poor reviews; while zero-defect, no-risk performance is lauded and praised. Most workers quickly learn that standing out from the pack makes them a target for managers who prefer blind obedience and loyalty and soon blend into the anonymity and safety of the herd. Not only does this create a nation of unhappy, disengaged, and frustrated workers, it also damages us economically and globally, especially in the face of other innovative, rapidly progressing countries such as Singapore, China, Vietnam, Israel, Brazil, and many others.

Ken Robinson, a British author, speaker, and advisor on the importance of education in the arts, speaks about how school systems kill creativity—how they focus on "fixing" what we're bad at, rather than celebrating and encouraging us in those areas where we each have our own unique brilliance. He advocates arts in the schools as a way of embracing alternative talents, rather than trying to force them into unfulfilling pre-set tracks. Crushing and devaluing the creative spirit prevents people from stepping fully into their strengths and that diminishes all of us in the long run. There is a way to earn money without dampening creativity—as we've seen both in the small anecdotes about Jessica Jackley and Angela Jia Kim, as well as in the case studies included in throughout this book.

But creativity is unfortunately not the norm. By the time most of us leave school behind us, we've learned not to employ creativity and critical thinking, not to challenge the status quo, but instead to please authority, to get the ultimate gold star—a promotion and material goods.

We have learned that if you are not "under" the radar and obeying all the "rules," you are a troublemaker, a malcontent, a loose cannon, and, as a result, a target. In school, you might have been labeled with ADD/ADHD and medicated, or kept in from recess because you couldn't contain your energy; in the workplace, you might be marginalized or fired.

Sound grim? To a certain extent it is! Tens of millions of unenthused, unengaged workers punch the clock, move their papers, file their TPS reports, count the hours until quitting time, and seek to anonymously avoid the stern gaze of their overseers. At the risk of depressing you further, in the next chapter we'll introduce what we term the "Donald Trump" approach to doing business, which is predicated on an "I win by you losing" or "I must win at all costs" mentality that's permeated all levels of American society – from business to politics to religion to sports – for the last 125 years.

"When you grow up, you tend to get told the world is the way it is and your life is just to live your life inside the world. 'Try not to bash the walls too much. Try to have a nice family, have fun, save a little money.'

That is a very limited life. Life can be much broader once you discover one simple fact: Everything around you that you call life was made up by people that were no smarter than you, and you can change it, you can influence it, you can build your own things that other people can use.

Once you learn that, you'll never be the same." - Steve Jobs

HERE'S WHAT WE ASK...

Stick with us through the next chapter (even if you feel like you want to take a shower at the end of it)...because we promise that there's light at the end of the tunnel. It's just that we need to understand where we've been to better inform us on the transformational power of possibilities presented by where we're going. Is that fair?

RECOMMENDED READING & MEDIA

☐ *Out of Our Minds: Learning to Be Creative,*
by Sir Ken Robinson

☐ **"Are Schools Killing Our Creativity,"** Sir Ken Robinson,
TED TALK: http://www.ted.com/talks/ken_robinson_says_
schools_kill_creativity.html

☐ **"Stop Stealing Dreams,"** Seth Godin,
http://www.squidoo.com/stop-stealing-dreams

NOTES

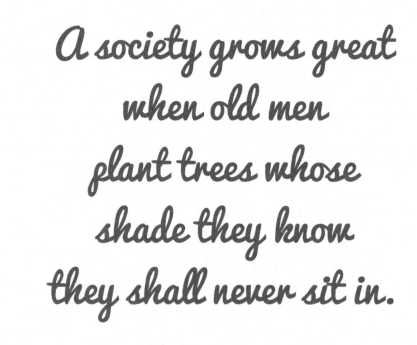

A society grows great when old men plant trees whose shade they know they shall never sit in.

– Greek Proverb

The Aggressive Business Model: Falling Behind by "Getting Ahead"

You're still here?

Excellent! Fasten your seat belts because we're about to pass through the darkest recesses of the American business psyche, exposing the unsavory neurons that brought us the Great Depression, the "Dot Com" Bomb, the epic housing and derivatives meltdown of 2007–09, and countless other scandals.

We believe events like these occur when the failed products of our broken education system collides with the "I win by you losing" or "I must win at all costs" business approach that plagues a small, but important, slice of Western business leaders.

This formula for disaster is created when you have several generations of business leaders who've emerged from some of our finest educational institutions with little exposure to true critical thinking, independent judgment, moral expectations, and values-based leadership.

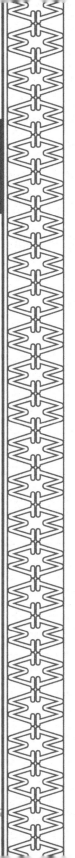

This formula focuses on one single imperative that defines career success: Maximize profits at all costs. The skewed compass that guides this attitude defends and even celebrates the end justifying the means and is sheathed by a seemingly impenetrable shield that protects the users against responsibility and consequences.

The enormous pressure to achieve short-term results so the next quarter will "look good" and maintain impressive bottom line results in a dangerously short-sighted obsession with squeezing every possible dime out of every transaction without a moment's thought given to possible unintended consequences or long-term adverse impact. This results in the increased willingness on the part of some to overlook our own ethical and moral boundaries in order to meet and exceed quarterly goals and profit margins (and therefore get ahead in your own career). In a world where the almighty dollar is your only compass, it is inevitable that you will lose sight of what is ethical, even if you start out with the best and most pure of intentions. The change is so gradual, so insidious, that you might not even realize how far past the line you've gone –"profitable" becomes synonymous with "acceptable," and the hazy gray area between right and wrong becomes extremely hard to identify.

Eventually, this blurring of ethical boundaries naturally leads to dishonesty, misrepresentation and downright fraud in the marketplace— what consumers don't know doesn't hurt them, and any move that makes money is fair game. The culture becomes one that is not interested in solving problems. Instead, the name of the game is preserving your own power and getting as much as you can as quickly as you can, for as long as you can, at any cost...including costs to your family, your community, the environment, and ironically, your career (ask Bernie Madoff what happened to his career.)

However, consumers and clients are becoming increasingly savvy about and concerned about the environment, responsible business practices, and a company's willingness to give back and be accountable when it makes mistakes. There is even a growing frustration with outsourcing, which takes jobs from Americans, hurts local businesses and can even put consumers at risk when manufactured in developing countries without the same health or environmental protections in place. The American Public is less and less willing to support greedy companies and short-term capitalists, even if it means higher prices for the goods and services they purchase. They are beginning to realize that their health and welfare are worth more than saving a few bucks.

And if you have a sole, self-serving purpose in your business life, that same attitude will seep into your personal life. Success in the corporate world means long hours, isolating you from your family and friends—which takes a definite toll on those relationships.

"SHORT-TERM CAPITALISTS"

Focusing on profits and power at the exclusion of everything else results in a narrowly focused track from which it's virtually impossible to deviate. If you live in this world, you are what Seth Godin calls "short-term capitalists," a group of business people with the mindset that they can act how they want in the present because they won't be there to face the consequences in the future.

As he states, "Short-term architecture means putting up a cheap building, a local eyesore, something that saves money now instead of building something for the long haul. The guys who put up the Parthenon in Rome weren't doing short-term anything. Hard to say that about a big box store. Short-term manufacturing ignores the side effects of pollution, bad design and worker impact because it's faster money in the short run to merely make the product (and the sale) in the most direct way possible."

Personal leadership
is the process of
keeping your
vision and values
before you and aligning
your life to be
congruent with them.

– **Stephen Covey**,
famed author of *The Seven Habits
of Highly Effective People*

Female entrepreneurs intuitively get Stephen Covey's view of leadership. Rejecting a male-dominated way of doing things and being guided by personal ethics – rather than avaricious business principles – is a more natural way for them to work. Embracing collaboration and cooperation is their natural path to success.

So, what's our action plan for moving away from this outdated model and embracing feminine energy?

First off, it's a recognition that feminine energy is about relationship, community, connection, and collaboration. It's about lifting up and paying it forward.

You must take this initiative at a personal level and make the conscious decision that you are going to operate from a conscious business perspective. After making this pledge to yourself, you must seek out others who are operating at this level and connect with them.

Jim Rohn, one of the original and most inspiring leaders of the life coaching movement, said, "You are the average of the five people you spend the most time with." This simple phrase holds immense power and wisdom, and it's a succinct explanation for what has happened to our culture.

When we surround ourselves with those who are invested in being morally upright and integrating their whole selves into their careers and into business, then we will take on those characteristics. Conversely, when we surround ourselves with those who are focused on shifting the lines between right and wrong to increase profits, careless of how their actions affect the company and its employees beyond basic profitability, we will become unscrupulous as well.

Take, for instance, James Arthur Ray—he started out with the best of intentions advocating the Law of Attraction to help others achieve success in business, but eventually he put profits above people, incorporating shady New Age practices into his programs and finally was convicted of three counts of negligent homicide for his involvement in three deaths in a "Spiritual Warrior" retreat involving a sweat lodge.

NOTES

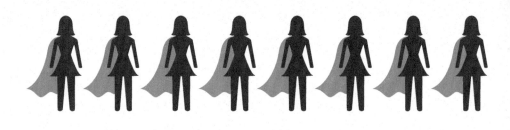

OUR SALVATION:
WHO WE ARE IS WHAT WE NEED

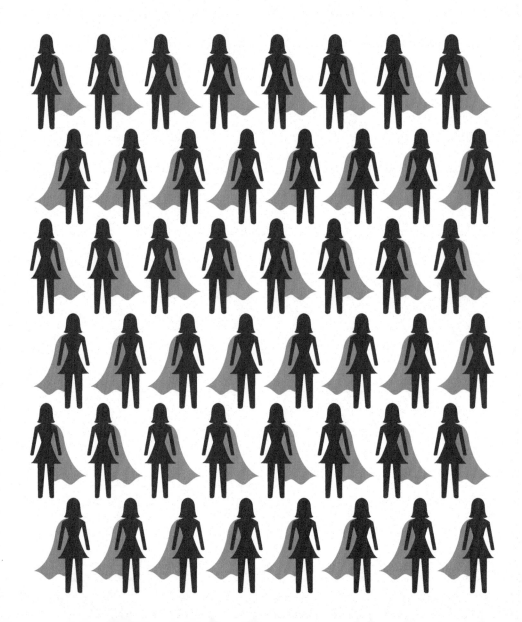

By now, you might feel a bit discouraged...or even depressed about the state of affairs in our educational system and our economy. But take heart! **We didn't lead you here to leave you here!** The real reason we wrote this book is because there is so much hope! Winston Churchill once said, "Those that fail to learn from history are doomed to repeat it." And in order to learn from our history, we had to know where we come from and why. But now we know, so the next step is finding out from where our salvation comes. **This is where it gets really exciting.** Over the next three chapters, we will explain in detail why YOU are the answer, and we will give you two vital foundational principles from which to build your superhero future. Heed the advice in these next three chapters and you will be poised and ready to flex your super powers and change the world!

Never doubt that
a small group of
thoughtful, committed
citizens can change
the world; indeed,
it's the only thing
that ever has.

— Margaret Mead

Change Is In the Air

Now for the good news: For every tragic story you hear about corrupt business practices, there's an equally uplifting story about entrepreneurs who have decided to do things differently.

They are implementing new practices in the workplace that will slowly but surely transform how America does business.

Here are some examples of companies doing things differently:

Zappos.com
Kiva.org
Toms
Stella & Dot
Virgin
Method
The Honest Co.

Now, these are mostly large companies. But none of them started out that way. And you don't have to hire hundreds of employees or generate millions in revenue to start making positive ripples in the business sector.

The Center for Women's Business Research did a study that showed that there are about **8 million women-owned enterprises in the U.S. alone, and that those enterprises generate approximately $3 trillion and create or maintain more than 23 million jobs — 16% of all U.S. employment.**

The World Bank has reported that on a global level, **women own or operate 25% to 33% of all private businesses.** Statistics show that women-owned enterprises grow faster than those owned by men and faster than businesses overall.

According to Forbes.com, **women are fast becoming THE job-creation engine for our country** – women start businesses and are responsible for an increase in new jobs at rates well beyond men and in a way that disproportionately exceeds their current contribution to U.S. employment.

The Bureau of Labor Statistics is predicting that by 2018, 15.3 million new jobs will be created. Do you want to know the best part? According to a new report by The Guardian Life Small Business Research Institute, women will create one-third, or 5.5 million new jobs!

Not only will women create these jobs, but the report predicts that **women will also be responsible for transforming the workplace from the male-dominated, hierarchical, exclusive "good ole boys" club of yesterday into a more "inclusive, horizontally-managed environment."** The report predicts that women business owners will create a very different work environment than the male-dominated work place we have all experienced. This will include characteristics such as a positive working environment and opportunities for all involved in the business, better pay and health care, better customer service and customer loyalty, a smarter focus on ideal clients, better collaboration and communication, and better long-term planning, including a succession plan and a solid retirement plan – not only for owners but for their employees.

As *Forbes* says so eloquently, "[T]his deeply engaged, inclusive, horizontal and diligent female-led approach to business management can be expected to counteract the top-down, command-and-control style long practiced by the male-dominant business establishment. Over the next decade, it will have a profound impact on the U.S. economy as female small-business owners create more opportunity for employees to grow in their jobs, encourage others to start their own small businesses and inspire a greater commitment to superior customer service and retention."

We don't know about you, but all of that data and those projections get us pretty darn excited. And you, as a female businesswoman, are uniquely situated to be a leader in this revolution. Because when there are no great leaders rising up over industry giants (as there most clearly have not been), then we must demonstrate a new kind of leadership within our businesses and communities, one business owner at a time—whether we have one employee or a thousand. On Main Street, we must begin to build our business structures with empathy, sympathy, and compassion for employees, customers, and ourselves.

IT IS TIME TO LEAD LIKE A WOMAN

We can save the world—if we turn our focus outward onto responsible business practices, considering others as well as ourselves, balancing the results-driven male consciousness with intuitive female empathy toward others – our clients and customers, our employees and our communities.

American businesswomen are uniquely situated to lead this revolution because they have the education, the freedom, the experience and now the vision and courage born of necessity in their own lives and businesses to be catalysts for bringing about the change that our business model so desperately needs.

WALT DISNEY

A grandaddy harbinger of change is that children's entertainment giant, Walt Disney. In *Creating Magic*, Lee Cockerel, the former vice president of operations for Walt Disney World resorts, writes about Disney's journey to a way of doing business that truly made their theme parks the happiest place on earth. He was one of the leaders within the organization that began pushing principles for happy employees and stellar customer service. When they began implementing these strategies in the 1990s, the company moved from a top-down management style where everyone was told what to do to an innovative program that created leaders across the entire company, from members of cleaning crews all the way up to high-ranking CEOs.

Management became focused on helping people understand that each position, no matter how insignificant it seemed. It gave managers the potential to exhibit leadership and make positive difference. **"We let it be known that managers and executives would not only be evaluated on their bottom line results, but on how those results were obtained. Everyone was now expected to live up to specific values and ideals,"** Cockerel writes. **"My way or the highway would be replaced by, 'What do you think?' As leaders, we are expected to encourage ongoing input and to show castmembers that their ideas were valued and that their needs were taken seriously."**

The directors at Disney saw that the way to get the best results was not just to focus on the bottom line, but rather on how you get there, keeping core values in mind. This strategy may have involved some financial sacrifices at the front end, but the eventual result was that the company's revenues skyrocketed.

Employees were happy and fulfilled and thus gave superlative customer service, which in turn made memorable experiences for visitors. Customers and employees became invested in the company, and as a result loyalty and profits grew—and now Disney has a rock-solid empire, as well as very low employee turnover.

TONY HSIEH, founder of Zappos.com

Tony Hsieh, who we've mentioned briefly before, changed the face of online retail by focusing not on the bottom line, but on making customers and employees **happy**. He employed both relationship marketing (focusing on customer retention) and loyalty-based marketing (high quality products lead to customer satisfaction and increased loyalty to the product), making customer service his number one priority. He was less concerned with making the initial sale than he was with making repeat sales to repeat customers.

As a result of this shift away from traditional "I win by you losing" competitive business strategy, his company soared—and now he has grossed over $1 billion annually in sales and served millions of customers, seventy-five percent of whom return to the company again and again.

His business philosophy? A set of ten core values that include **"Build a Positive Team and Family Spirit," "Do More with Less,"** and **"Deliver WOW Through Service."**

For a list of all ten values, see Super Power One, Authenticity, later in the book.

The Mission-Driven Super Hero

You don't have to hire hundreds of employees or generate millions in revenue to start making positive ripples in the business sector. You can start in your own backyard. The first step in joining the Wonder Women revolution will be to create a mission statement (discussed further in Super Power One, Authenticity), one that integrates your whole person—spiritually, emotionally, intellectually—and then stick to it, even if it means your bottom line isn't quite as impressive as you hoped. Demonstrating integrity in your business practices will pay off in the end—for you, your customers, and your employees. That is what companies like Zappos and Disney have done, and they have not suffered financially for it. **In fact, it is because of their mission statements and a consistent commitment to living by them that they are so successful.**

Our culture is pretty repressive emotionally and spiritually, and it takes courage to face that and choose to live a different way. Breaking away from the male-dominated business mindset won't happen in six months, and there's no magic wand to create change—**but making the change is an investment in the rest of your life, a change of course that can significantly and positively impact your children, families, and community.**

Your actions will have a ripple effect, and the solution to perpetrating change is not continuing to trudge along in the status quo of old-school corporate America. The change requires starting your own business, continuing your business with a change in tactic, or working for a business owner who **leads like a woman** (see the next chapter for how to do this!) This shift won't necessarily be easy, but if you look around your community, reaching out and connecting with like-minded people, it can be done.

So how do you do it? How do you become a real super hero, a wonder woman who will help save the world? In the next two chapters, we promised you two vital foundational principles that you need to begin to build your super hero profile. Then, in the third section of this book, we are going to share with you the top seven super powers that you will need to step into your real power as a woman business owner. **So if you are ready to change the world, read on!**

NOTES

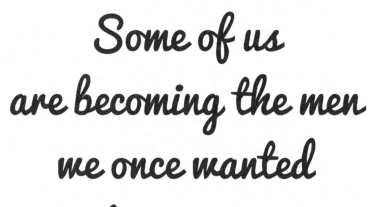

Some of us
are becoming the men
we once wanted
to marry.

– Gloria Steinem

Stop Being Guys – Lead Like a Girl

Despite the challenges we still face – such as less pay per dollar on average and less promotion opportunity than their equivalently situated male counterparts – women now undeniably have more opportunities in business than ever before—but at what price?

The only way in which women have known how to access the business world has been on men's terms—by mimicking their business ethic and adopting their values.

Women's entrance into the workplace has come at the severing of what makes women special, the negation of the intuitive, unique feminine energy that could be used to transform and benefit business as it currently stands.

Women's entrance into the workplace has come at the SEVERING of what makes women special, the NEGATION of the INTUITIVE, unique feminine energy that could be used to transform and benefit BUSINESS as it currently stands.

In the 1950s, women were taught to seek out a man who was financially responsible and who had a good job, someone who could support them and their future children in a respectable middle-class life. However, even before that, a shift in consciousness about women's roles had started to occur. During World War II, when most eligible men were drafted and deployed, women had begun to step into traditionally male roles in the workplace, taking on responsibilities previously barred to them. These women ran and supported their households at the same time. It was the era of **Rosie the Riveter**.

Early on, these women left home to work in the name of patriotic sacrifice. But for many women, this entry into a previously male sphere was a heady experience—and one they wanted more of. When the war ended and the men returned, ready to reassume their places as masters of the hearth and workplace, women were not so eager to give up the toehold they had gained. Their desire to work became less about patriotism and more about personal fulfillment and freedom.

The civil rights revolution of the 1960s led to increased rights for women and minorities, and by the 1970s and 1980s, women were struggling to shed their femininity in order to prove themselves among men in the workforce. **They did this by acting like men**. They cut their hair, donned power suits, and left their motherhood at the door. And they made tremendous strides.

The women today who have such freedom to build businesses and careers of their own are standing on the shoulders of these early, courageous, career women.

However, despite the challenges still faced, such as less pay per dollar on average and less promotion opportunity than their equivalently situated male counterparts, women now undeniably have more opportunities in business than ever before—but at what price? Women have had to assume masculine stances and attitudes in the workplace, communicating in a brusque, typically male way so that they don't stand out. **Being "one of the guys" has been the path to promotion and success—and for most women this unfortunately means leaving a huge part of themselves behind, including valuable feminine traits such as compassion and empathy.**

This narrow conception of how success must be achieved in the business world is doing ourselves as individuals and our identity as a country a great disservice.

On a primal level, most women are wired to desire cooperation and collaboration. Most women are naturally inclined towards caretaking and finding positive solutions that allow everyone to benefit, rather than just one side winning at the expense of the other. Although women have been increasingly conditioned to ignore and reject feminine energy, for most, this doesn't feel natural. **In the end, many women begin to experience a serious dissonance between their work and home personas.**

The solution? Women have to stop acting like guys and start leading like women.

▶ DON'T LEAN IN! ◀

But HOW do you lead like a woman? What does it mean? There is a lot of debate about this, especially Marissa Mayer's recent decision as CEO of Yahoo! to order all telecommuting workers back to the office, or Facebook COO Sheryl Sandberg's campaign around her new book, *Lean In*. There's a strong tradition in our culture of conditioning men to embrace their manliness, to take a no-holds-barred, never-back-down attitude.

Little boys on the playground hurl "Don't be a girl!" or "You throw like a girl!" as an insult, and that mindset deepens and persists on into adulthood.

Often, being a woman has had the connotation of being weak, emotional and even ineffective, while being a man means being forceful and assertive. **The thinking goes that women stand back, men achieve success.** As each of you ladies know, nothing could be further from the truth. But the idea of it is so prevailing that Sheryl Sandberg's entire premise in her new book is that women need to lean in toward opportunities instead of leaning back.

What bothers us about this mindset is that it comes from the assumption that the male definition of success is unequivocally what success is:

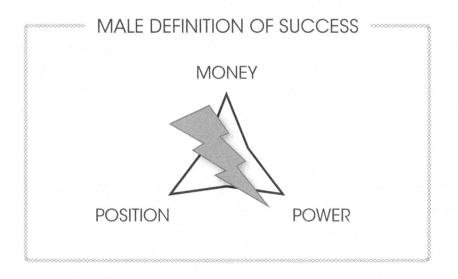

MALE DEFINITION OF SUCCESS

MONEY

POSITION   POWER

There is so much speculation about why there aren't more women sitting on boards of major companies, or serving as chief executive officers. **It isn't because women lean back from success.** This is particularly puzzling when Fortune 500 companies with the highest representation of women board members attain greater financial performance, according to a recent study by Catalyst*. It is because on an inherent, gut level, women know the truth about what success really is. And as long as women try to fit into the old school way of defining success, they will always be miserable.

It is very difficult to lean into opportunities that conflict with our values and priorities. Women can't lead when they don't believe in the end goal. LEADING LIKE A WOMAN ISN'T ABOUT THE SAME END GOAL.

* http://catalyst.org

Yes, women are capitalists and want to make money. But women also want to bring their humanity to all they do. At their core, if women lead as they are wired to do, they lead with compassion, intuition, collaboration, connection and all while holding their families, communities and the world in trust.

Anything less is like a fish trying to climb a tree.

And it is very hard to use your humanity to lead an organization with shareholders and male counterparts who are firmly entrenched in the old way of building and growing a company and a profit. THAT is why most women lean back.

LEAD LIKE A WOMAN

So we ask you again: How do you lead like a woman? Well, you do it by either having the courage to take the old system on and prove that leading like a woman makes a difference. Or, you start your own company and do it your way, like so many women are doing.

Whichever path you choose, **never forget to lead like a woman.** For the remainder of this book, we are going to give you a step-by-step road map to leading like a woman. But in short, don't be afraid to do it because you fear it will hurt your success. With all the companies succeeding while valuing humanity and human connection and happiness, we know for certain that bringing feminine energy to the boardroom or business and making a profit are not mutually exclusive. **You can have it all.**

Women just have to re-engage with the feminine, softening back to a natural point of balance without losing the assertive positive points of masculine power. Because technology has created so many opportunities in today's world, women can more easily facilitate this change in business—in large part because there aren't as many barriers to entry. In fact, you can easily create your own opportunities and setting model business behavior by starting your own businesses.

Bringing feminine energy to the boardroom and excelling in business are not mutually exclusive.

But to be on board with this new way of doing business, we must overcome the mindset that being soft means you will overlook numbers and metrics and go easy on employees, resulting in wasted assets and decreased productivity. You can still make large profits; you can still have expectations of people. Bringing feminine energy to the boardroom and excelling in business are not mutually exclusive. You can balance feminine and masculine energy without it negatively affecting your business and bottom line.

In the end, it's a win-win situation: the powerful woman leader who can bring everyone along to share in her success, without devaluing those who work beneath or stepping on anyone else. You can still bring the male energy to the table, of course, and male energy does have its benefits, as discussed in Chapter 1; but be open and receptive to the benefits of feminine energy. You can achieve far more in a shorter period of time if you balance the two energies, using them as the situation demands to find the most effective solution.

Many women strike out on their own as entrepreneurs because of the physical and mental toll of juggling a family, personal needs, and business responsibilities. Merging the best aspects of both man and woman is the first step to creating real life Wonder Women and Wonder Men, and will go a long way toward helping you achieve inner peace and happiness, as well as the outer trappings of success.

Men can also turn to embracing their feminine energy. There's a strong tradition in our culture of conditioning men to embrace their manliness, to take a no-holds-barred, never-back-down attitude. Little boys on the playground hurl "Don't be a girl!" as an insult, and that mindset continues on into adulthood. Being a woman means being weak and ineffective, while being a man means being forceful and assertive. Women stand back, men achieve success.

And yet we can see from countless examples and know on a personal level that this is just not the case. So how do we combat this attitude? It's an uphill battle but not insurmountable, especially considering the extensive social and business proof that yes, women can succeed and even surpass men in the workplace—and they can do so on their own terms.

As men see that this way of living – one that embraces feminine energy and balances it with the masculine for the most effective business plan – can bring equal if not more success in business, it can give them the courage to say, "I am not a woman, but I recognize that women have a lot to offer the workplace, and I can become more successful by recognizing and embracing feminine energy in my own career and business."

GUYS!

NOTES

NOTES

There is a special
place in hell
reserved for
women who
don't help
other women.

– Madeleine Albright

Ladies: Stop Tearing Each Other Down

Starting your own business is a hard decision, one that involves a lot of soul-searching and a willingness to face the unknown, and it's almost impossible to succeed without a strong support group around you.

Ideally, you will find that support group from within your current group of friends, family and colleagues. It is natural to believe that the people you know best and who love you would rally behind you when you are trying to forge a new path for yourself. Unfortunately, it is rare to find yourself already surrounded with the people you will need. Most entrepreneurs learn quickly that they have to find a new "tribe" for the support and encouragement they need. But just looking to other women is not necessarily the right answer either. It should be, and in an ideal world, women would always have each other's backs.

Unfortunately, it's very likely that you'll encounter more naysayers than cheerleaders.

And many of these naysayers will be women...

"Who does she think she is?"

"She is a terrible mother..."

"She isn't ambitious enough..."

"I can't imagine leaving my kids alone to be raised by someone else..."

"I can't imagine having to be home all day with the kids..."

"She might be smart, but did you see what she was wearing?"

But wait! Shouldn't your fellow women be supporting you in achieving your dreams, rather than trying to dissuade you? In an ideal world, women would support and lift each other up, taking joy in each other's successes and easing each other's failures. But we all have our own stories to share about how that is not always the case.

Today's society lauds strong female figures, yes—think Oprah—but it also often roots for their downfall—think Hillary Clinton or Carly Fiorina. And it's probably no coincidence that one of those women is powerful in a "safe" medium, entertainment, while the others are powerful in politics and business, traditionally male-dominated spheres. **And many of women's most virulent critics are other women.** They criticize other women for being too feminine, not being feminine enough, choosing to have children, choosing not to have children, for having a nanny, for sending their kids to preschool, for working too hard, for not leaning in, for the way they walk and talk and look and act.

One thing women get most virulently attacked over is how "selfish" it is to pursue a career while having children, as if working to support one's family counts as a form of neglect. Women in our society are supposed to walk a very fine line and do it flawlessly, or they get thrown to the wolves, subjected to barbed criticisms and judgment. Women are supposed to raise the kids, plan the family events, buy all the holiday gifts, remember everyone else's birthdays and anniversaries, be there for their kids when they are sick or have school activities, attend all of their kids' plays, soccer games, and music recitals, all while keeping a spotlessly clean house. Women are supposed to keep everything running smoothly. However, in today's economy, most women also have to work—and work really hard.

So, women are expected to tack a career onto all of our other activities and do everything well and without complaining. As a result of this, many women feel like they are drowning or on the verge of a nervous breakdown because of the weight of expectations and responsibilities they face. Of course, there are evolved men out there who genuinely carry half (or more) of the non-work responsibilities and are actual team players at home. But generally, that's not how the situation unfolds, and when a woman pulls back from a few responsibilities at home—the laundry's undone, the groceries still need to be bought—in order to pursue a career, she's vilified.

However, when a man works to build wealth and an empire of his own, he is touted as brilliant, ambitious, a real "go-getter," a winner. We respect and admire men who try to have it all. You will rarely hear in the media any criticism of men for not doing their share at home or not spending time with their kids.

Not so for women. If a woman is ambitious and is trying to build an empire, she often gets labeled as a bad mother and bad person. She is called a narcissist, irresponsible, vain. She is accused of not having her priorities straight and not loving her kids.

But a mother has to earn a living just the same as a father, and there's no rule that says a mother's career can't be fun and fulfilling – that the only true fulfillment lies at home.

If you are struggling with guilt or are suffering from active criticism from your work schedule or career plans, take a long hard look at this double standard and try to remove yourself from its grip. All women experience guilt, but if you are like the majority of women, you have to earn a living. Period. End of story. And if you're going to work an eight to ten hour day, you're much better off (and so are your daughters and sons) if you are doing something you love and get excited about. If you are a mom and you are fulfilled and successful, you provide a fantastic role model for your children, help support their self-esteem, and teach them how to successfully juggle the responsibilities that they will have later in life, while also taking care of themselves. If your children know you are happy, engaged in your life and enjoying the ride, you are giving them permission to live life in the same way.

Of course even if you don't have children, you'll still face judgment and comments about your ability to have a career. Maybe you're a "dumb blonde," or you're engaged and so of course once you get married you'll stop working.

And the criticism doesn't stop there. Once you start your own business, you'll also face the comments of others who say that you just won't be able to make it on your own, that you are taking too many risks, that you don't have enough experience, that your ideas will never work.

At first, it's easy to respond to these attacks with hurt and resentment, **but it's important to understand that the potential of you – as a successful women – is a mirror of chances others will not take, and of risks they fear.** If you experience judgment, take a step back from the hostile situation. Use empathy and compassion to see whether the attacks come from either a good place or a place of jealousy. If it's a person close to you, realize that they might fear how failure will affect you, or fear what will happen to your family if you don't have a regular paycheck. If the remarks come from place of jealousy, it might really be because they wish they had the strength and bravery to pursue their own dreams. **Either way, if you understand their motivation you can defuse its impact on you.**

Conversely, don't judge others. If you don't know firsthand what's going on in a woman's life, up-level your integrity and make the decision that you're not going to participate in that discussion. Develop an awareness of whom you are and what matters, then give other women the chance to do the same. Don't presume you can see inside their hearts and homes—instead, wish success for them.

Let's start having some empathy and compassion for each other.

If you are feeling the jealousy yourself, stop and ask yourself why you are choosing to have that experience. More often than not, it goes deeper than you think. Why are you so jealous of that particular woman's success? Has she achieved something you've been afraid to reach for? How can you use her as an inspiration rather than a source of discontent?

Women are amazing creatures who really can multi-task and do it brilliantly. If you don't know from first-hand knowledge about what is going on in another woman's life, refrain from perpetuating the ugly and unfair double standard.

Another key way to combat others' negativity is to seek out a community of people who will encourage and support what you do, as well as find appropriate mentors—both of which will be addressed in Super Power Optimism, later in this book.

> In addition, running a successful business is WORK! The old adage that most overnight successes are 10 years in the making is very true. Enduring success requires dedication, building the right team, focusing on what you - as the business owner - do best, and surrounding yourself with cheerleaders who will root for you through thick and thin.
>
> Seek those supporters out and, more importantly, when you start achieving success, be that cheerleader for other women in business!

ACTION ITEM CHECKLIST

☐ I will stop jumping to instant judgments of women who have chosen a different path than I have.

☐ I will encourage other women and think positive thoughts for them, wishing them the same success I wish for myself.

☐ If I feel jealousy for another woman, I will examine the reasons why I am experiencing that emotion, instead of projecting my negative feelings onto her choices.

NOTES

HOW WESTERN WOMEN
WILL SAVE THE WORLD

Now that you know what the root of the problem is, and know what part you can play in changing things for the better, it is time to give you our list of the top **seven Super Powers you need in order to be a true Wonder Woman in business (and in life!)**

This next section will take you through each Super Power:

★ 1. Authenticity

★ 2. Sustainability

★ 3. Integrity

★ 4. Curiosity

★ 5. Creativity

★ 6. Optimism

★ 7. Courage

By the end of the book, you will be ready to don your cape and fly!

1

au·then·tic·i·ty, n.

1. The quality or condition of being authentic, trustworthy, or genuine;

2. True to one's own personality, spirit, or character;

3. *The Wonder Women Way:* Being true to yourself so that what you do necessarily includes significance, purpose, decisiveness, self-confidence, and balance.

AUTHENTICITY

Know Thyself

Start as you mean to end up – or as Plato said, "Know Thyself."

There is nothing more important in this new economy than knowing who you are at your core, what makes you tick, what you are exceptionally good at, and why you get out of bed in the morning.

And for most of us, these answers might not be immediately clear, especially in a culture where we have been taught to fit into a box or a cookie-cutter mold of what a successful person looks like. But in order to really be a true Wonder Woman, it is critical that you slow down and take the time to know yourself well.

Life isn't about finding yourself. Life is about creating yourself.
– George Bernard Shaw

We call this first super power AUTHENTICITY. If you come from a place of being authentic, you will find that you will have clarity on what your purpose and path should be, and everything else will become so much easier.

Now, this isn't just a pep talk about "just be yourself," or "just do your best." No, what we are talking about is much larger and much more profound. We have found that people who build their businesses from a place of authenticity have an entire arsenal of tools from which to make decisions about how and when to proceed.

Knowing yourself will ultimately enable you to be a true success, and by that we mean that you will know that your work has significance and purpose, you will be better equipped to make quick and necessary decisions about your business, you will gain self-confidence and direction And you will get much closer to achieving balance in your daily life. Pretty awesome, huh? And the first step to getting all that is to spend the next chapter with us learning how to know yourself. If this is a Super Power you want, then read on!

We encourage you to set aside a good 2–3 hours to really work through the next few exercises. Shut off your phone, don't check email or the internet and try to focus on this without interruption, if possible.

WHAT DO YOU THINK ABOUT?

Most of us naturally spend a majority of our time drawn to the things we love, are passionate about or that make us happy. If we aren't able to spend as much time as we would like doing those things, then we surely spend a lot of time thinking about them. So, the first step to developing your Super Power of Authenticity is to be very deliberate in noticing how you spend your time, attention, energy and money. What things do you day dream about? What do you long for in your life? If there are people whose lives you admire, what do those lives look like and what specifically about those experiences or achievements do you admire?

WHAT DO YOU WANT?

Once you have some clarity about what takes up your thought processes and day dreams, you can then move more tangibly into getting clarity about what you want. **Having clarity on what you want is a vital part of building a business that supports you and your life.** If you don't go to the trouble of getting clear on this, you could end up with a business that you serve and that doesn't give you the freedom you need to have the life you really want. So, know what you want. What will your life look like when you "arrive"? Get clarity on that now, before you are beholden to a board, and investors, and creditors.

There is no wrong way to build a business, and you need to be sure you know what you want before you start handing over control or say-so to anyone else. This includes specific things, like **what time of the day do you want to start working? What time do you want to be done? Do you mind working evenings and weekends? Do you want to be free to be there for your kids sporting events, performances and teacher conferences? Do you want to take vacations? What kind of salary do you want to draw?**

WHAT DOES YOUR IDEAL LIFE (AND BUSINESS) LOOK LIKE?

The kind of life you want will help you determine your business structure. Here are some of the key considerations:

• Are you going to build a lifestyle business or a business you can sell or grow into an empire, for example?

• What sort of work hours will your product or service require of you?

• Will you need a formal office, a virtual office, or will you be a road warrior with a great frequent flyers' program?

• Will you be building a traditional team with W-2 employees, a virtual team of vendors and independent contractors, or a hybrid team consisting of both? How big will your team be?

As the late Stephen Covey recommends in Habit 2 of *The Seven Habits of Highly Effective People*, **"Begin with the end in mind."** You need to develop a clear sense of exactly what you are heading into—will you have the life you've always dreamed of, or will you spiral into frustration and exhaustion because you just can't keep up with all of your commitments? If your priority is to be home every day when your children get home from school, but your business model is set up for seventy-hour weeks or requires you to travel several weeks out of the month, you're probably not moving in the right direction.

Conversely, if you crave the thrill of frequent travel but are constantly tied to an office or bogged down in managing a large team, you'll also be unhappy. Your passion for your business needs to be able to co-exist and dovetail with what you want out of your personal life, as well—or you'll end up pulled in different directions, not any better off than before you escaped the corporate race.

{ MARKET NEEDS VS. MARKET WANTS }

Let's say you've had a major challenge in your life, figured out a way to overcome that challenge, and now have a great idea for a product or service that can help others overcome a similar challenge. You're fired up because you're convinced the market absolutely NEEDS what your offering and you just KNOW your product/service is a "can't miss" success. Unfortunately, success in the market isn't determined by what everyone needs…it's dictated by what the market WANTS. If we all did what we NEED to do, we'd all be wealthy, fit, and living with our soul-mate!

Before spending tens or hundreds of thousands of dollars developing a product/service, take time to analyze the marketplace to see where it might fit. You may see a hole in existing offerings that needs to be filled, like Tony Hsieh with Zappos.com, or you might discover an entirely unmet need to develop. Either way, you must have a practical basis to go on, and you must stay grounded in reality. As our friend Larry Broughton, serial entrepreneur and CEO of multiple companies, including broughtonHOTELS and Broughton Advisory says, "Reality is your friend. There are very few truly original ideas in the market and if a product/service doesn't exist in the market, there could be a very good reason...like nobody wants it."

It's usually much easier to succeed with a product/service that's a twist on something that's already out there, that the market already wants and is buying than it is to create a new market. The more education you have to do before someone will buy your product/service, the longer it will take you to achieve success and the more resources you'll need to sustain your business until you can educate enough people to buy.

Unfortunately, we've seen many passionate entrepreneurs put themselves in the poor house by violating this cardinal rule: If the market doesn't want it, the market won't buy it. This is a primary area where having the right coach or mentor is invaluable (we'll discuss this in greater depth in **Super Power Six, Optimism**). Having someone with the right experience and knowledge who has walked the path ahead of you, that you can bounce ideas off of and get constructive feedback from, is essential. Remember, if passion were all it took, we'd all be millionaires!

A good way to know whether an idea is a viable one is to ask yourself, "Does my business solve a problem?" If it does, then ask yourself three questions developed by Craig Stull, Phil Myers and David Meerman Scott, co-authors of *Tuned In: Uncover the Extraordinary Opportunities That Lead to Business Breakthroughs:*

1) Is that probelm urgent?
2) Is it pervasive in the marketplace?
3) Are buyers willing <u>and able</u> to pay to have that problem solved?

Even after you've done your research and found a potentially successful product/service, don't just assume that hanging out a shingle will draw customers to your door. You'll still need to be savvy about positioning yourself as an expert as well as in marketing your new business. Success is a complex interplay of factors, and there's no one-size-fits all approach. You can get more information on monetizing your idea in our discussion of **Super Power Four, Curiosity.**

KNOW WHAT YOUR BRILLIANCE IS

In other words, what can you do really, really well? Everyone has some area where they shine. Before you become a Wonder Woman or Man, you must devote time to finding your unique brilliance zone—the special gift that you can give to the business world. This unique brilliance zone, which is dictated by your basic emotional and intellectual make-up, is the linchpin of your success or failure as an entrepreneur, and yet it rarely gets attention from the popular business coaches. Despite a lack of focus on it, it's worth exploring deeply and with dedication.

DISCOVERING AND EMPHASIZING YOUR STRENGTHS

Every single one of us has different passions, different hot buttons, and different reactions to certain stimuli. It's what makes us individuals—and it's why there's no one-size-fits all to approaching a business. How you're "built," so to speak, determines how you will respond to certain challenges—an important factor in determining how successful you will become long-term. It's not enough just to say, "I'm a good baker, so I should open a cupcake store," or "I love tennis, so I'm going to design a new and improved caddy." There's more to discovering your intrinsic skills than that, and there's much more that goes into analyzing the market for your product or service!

Your unique brilliance zone is a complex interplay of your skills, your passion, your Conative make-up, and your life experiences—and discovering exactly who you are and what you want creates a strong foundation for your business.

WAIT! WHAT THE HECK IS YOUR "CONATIVE MAKE-UP?"

Conative is from "conation," which is "the part of mental process or behavior having to do with striving, including desire and volition." * To find your true conative make-up, we strongly urge you to put this book down and take the Kolbe A™ Index and Strengthsfinder 2.0 assessments immediately. They only take about 20 minutes each to complete, and provide invaluable insight into your natural skills and problem-solving modus operandi (M.O.).

You can take the Kolbe A Index by going to www.Kolbe.com or connect with a Kolbe Certified Consultant (like Phil). The basic Kolbe A Index assessment is $49.95.

You can take the Strengthsfinder 2.0 by visiting the Gallup Strengths Center at www.gallupstrengthscenter.com. The basic Strengthsfinder 2.0 assessment is $9.95.

*www.dictionary.com

4 KOLBE A
Index action modes !

FACT FINDER: GATHER AND SHARE INFORMATION

FOLLOW THRU: ARRANGE AND DESIGN

QUICK START: DEAL WITH RISK AND UNCERTAINTY

IMPLEMENTOR: HANDLE SPACE AND TANGIBLES

The **Kolbe A Index** assessment determines your *Conative* strength in four key action modes and determines which mode(s) you operate from to initiate solutions, accommodate, or prevent problems. The Kolbe Action Modes® include **FACT FINDER, FOLLOW THRU, QUICK START,** and **IMPLEMENTOR** (please note that Implement is used as noun – as in tool or object – as opposed to a verb referring to getting something done), as shown on the table on the following page.

Your strength in each Kolbe Action Mode® determines how you instinctually take action anytime you are expending mental energy. Understanding how you're built from a Kolbe perspective will tell you exactly where you should – and shouldn't – be focusing your time and energy in your business. Although each Kolbe Action Mode® is measured on a scale of 1 to 10, the numbers – whether high or low – are neither good nor bad; they just are.

Each Kolbe Action Mode® is divided into three zones, determined by your results in each Action Mode:

- Prevent Problems: 1–3
- Accommodate: 4–6
- Initiate Solutions: 7–10

12 KOLBE A
Index zones!

The diagram below details each of the 12 possible Kolbe A Index zones.

Fact Finder	Follow Thru	Quick Start	Implementor
Simplify	Adapt	Stabilize	Imagine
Explain	Maintain	Modify	Restore
Specify	Systematize	Improvise	Build

My Kolbe score: _____

Ah-Ha! From my Kolbe score: _____

_____

_____

_____

_____

In the excerpt of the Kolbe A Index below, note that this person initiates solutions from the Fact Finder mode, is accommodating in both the Follow Thru and Quick Start mode, and prevents problems from the Implementor mode. As a result, they are very detailed oriented and can be relied upon to handle extensive research (8 Fact Finder). They'll also be pretty good working with systems and business processes (6 Follow Thru), although they shouldn't be relied on to build systems from scratch. They won't be comfortable dealing with too much risk, uncertainty or changing priorities (4 Quick Start). Finally, they'll use vision and imagination (2 Implementor) instead of building physical models.

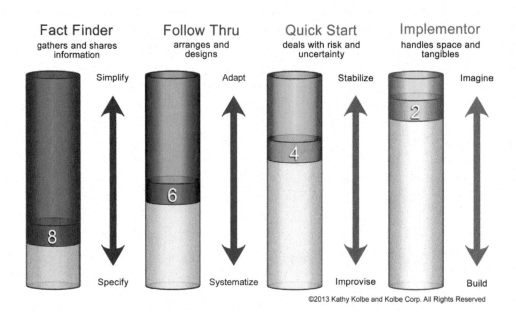

Why is understanding your Conative strengths so important? Once you're out of your formative years – typically by age 15 to 19 – your conative strengths are essentially part of your internal DNA and won't change later in life, barring a traumatic brain injury or other physiological change to your brain (in fact, more recent studies show that Conative strengths are primarily formed as early as ages 5-7). In addition, your Conative make-up is pretty unique, with only about 5% of the people across the globe having a similar Kolbe A Index result.

The Strengthsfinder 2.0 assessment, developed by the Gallup organization, is a great adjunct to the Kolbe A Index and identifies your top 5 themes (strengths) out of 34 they've identified through studying millions of people (as of June 2013, nearly 9 million people have taken Strengthsfinder 2.0). The results not only identify your top 5 strengths - such as Activator, Ideation, Learner, Maximizer, Positivity, Strategic, and Woo; they provide detailed tips on how to leverage your strengths for better productivity, team work, and job satisfaction.

A precise and crystal-clear understanding of who you are is a key pillar of launching your business. Focusing on, operating within, and leveraging your strengths leads to sustainable success, higher energy levels, enduring engagement, and – ultimately – a happier you!

Attempting to operate against your strengths is literally like trying to oppose Mother Nature and will leave you frustrated, exhausted, stuck, and usually ends in failure. Remember, you're far more than just the collection of jobs on your résumé.

Your unique blend of experience, personality, and Conative abilities will determine what specific activities you should focus on in your business, what type of team you need to build, which business strategies will empower, and which strategies will likely make you fall on your face. This is powerful, life changing, liberating stuff!

Discovering your unique brilliance zone will also help you structure your business to provide the best chance for success. Let's say you're incredibly personable and a genius at sales, but that you're also hopelessly unorganized and can't seem to follow systems to save your life. If you hate spending time trying to put things in order and aren't very good at it, you'll waste enormous amounts of time and mental energy trying to get organized (because "good" business owners are organized) and continuously beat yourself up about it.

Unfortunately, if you focus time and energy on things that you're not very good at and/or really dislike doing, there will be at least two very undesirable outcomes:

UNDESIRABLE OUTCOME #1:
Entrepreneurship will be a constant struggle that will suck the very life out of you.

UNDESIRABLE OUTCOME #2:
You will rob others, who love to do and excel in the areas you suck at, of the opportunity to thrive, make a living and contribute meaningfully to your team.

The solution? Delegate, delete, or defer anything that you aren't great at and love to do (we'll address this further with **SUPER POWER 5: CREATIVITY**). Low-value, $15-to-30/hour tasks distract far too many entrepreneurs while key strategic business development initiatives go undone.

Of course, you'll wear a lot of hats when you first start off, and you won't spend every second doing things you're perfectly suited for. That's how real life works. That said, the idea is to focus in on the highest and best use of your time, and outsource, delegate, delete, and defer everything else as quickly as possible to a virtual, traditional, or hybrid team. Otherwise, you'll wind up procrastinating on or avoiding the things you dislike or aren't good at and drop the ball in one or more important business areas.

In an ideal situation, you should spend 70 to 80 percent of your time as a business owner operating in your strengths. If you make this a priority, you'll be astounded at how many other things in your business fall into line. Once you've identified your core entrepreneurial strengths, you also want to determine the kind of life you want to live and the kind of business you want to have.

Use the next exercise to find your brilliance. Most people spend less than 20–30% of their time operating in their areas of greatest strength and ability. This is enormously costly to organizations and to individuals. Make it your mission to spend more time in your personal brilliance zone!

"SOMETIMES I HAVE TO REMIND MYSELF THAT I DON'T HAVE TO DO WHAT EVERYONE ELSE IS DOING."

- Source Unknown

MISSION: *Finding your brilliance!*

The goal of this exercise is to hone in on the 3-5 activities/tasks that you both excel at and love.

STEP 1: Starting in the DOING column, take 3-5 minutes to write down at least 20 tasks you do hourly, daily, weekly, monthly, quarterly, or annually in your business. Don't self-filter or analyze, just write and capture as many items as you can.

STEP 2: Now, move only those tasks which you are truly really **GREAT AT** to the center column. Be honest! If others have consistently marvelled at how good you are at a particular task, or if it's something that people pay you to do because you excel at it, then move it here. Resist the urge to move a task because you *should, have to, or ought to.*

STEP 3: Finally, move only those tasks which you truly **LOVE DOING** into third column. How much love are we talking about? If you won a multi-gazillion dollar lottery tomorrow and the only stipulation was that you had to do something productive each day, kind of love. Be really selective, aim for about 3-5 activities here.

BONUS! Go back to the first column and circle the two activities/tasks that you really detest. You know the ones we're talking about...the ones that you'll procrastinate on starting as long as possible and then want to take a nap 5 minutes after starting them. We challenge you to figure out a way to delegate, delete, or defer that activity within the next 2 weeks. That's right! Get rid of it...because it's sucking the life out of you!

If you work with a team of 5 or more people, have everyone on your team do this exercise - including the bonus step - and then compile the list of 10 or so activities/tasks that everyone can't stand doing. Voila...you've just created the position description for your next hire. Find someone who is thrilled to do the tasks that everyone else on the team hates. They are out there...we promise!

Need help finding your brilliance? Refer to the sample on the right.
Download our worksheet on our website www.wonderwomenbook.com

DOING	GREAT AT!	LOVE DOING!
Invoicing clients	Replying to email	Social media
Replying to email	Social media	Engaging new clients
Ordering office supplies	Engaging new clients	Developing new product
Book keeping	Developing new product	
Social media	Managing people	
Engaging new clients		
Developing new product		
Managing people		

WHAT DO YOU STAND FOR?

What kind of impact do you want to have on the world? Have the courage to build that into your company's mission statement. There is nothing worse than building something only to find yourself pushed out of it because it wasn't a good fit for you any longer. Ask Andrew Mason, the founder of Groupon, how he feels about this after he was recently fired from the company he founded. As Lewis Carroll, the beloved author said,

"If you don't know where you are going, any road will get you there."

We assume you are here because you want to do something different, something meaningful, something successful and something that will give you financial success. Know where you are headed personally and build that into your daily activities as a mission statement. And then make sure that all you do has that end game in mind. If you don't, your business could turn into something that is very different from what you wanted. Be the leader of your vision and have the courage to set your course.

A personal mission statement distills a clear sense of who you are and why you're doing what you do, all in a few succinct sentences. It's both a starting off point and constant guidance for your entrepreneurial journey. It needs to be about more than money or quarterly sales—it needs to be imbued with meaning for your life.

MISSION STATEMENTS

These mission statements are from companies we admire, love and think are doing a good job. We will work on your company's mission statement in the next chapter, but for now, use these as inspiration to craft your **personal** mission statement.

No mission is too lofty, and none is too trivial. Some of may be called to run a non-profit, while others may be called to design textiles, or teach children, or create a program that changes the world. Or we may be called on to be the best mother, sister, aunt, or daughter that we can be. There's no right or wrong vision for your life!

STELLA AND DOT

TO GIVE EVERY WOMAN THE MEANS TO STYLE HER OWN LIFE.
We get great joy out of designing irresistible jewelry. And yet, jewelry is just the tangible expression of something much greater we are creating. We have a vision of the world where STRONG WOMEN LIVE BOLD and joyful lives. They know what they want and they work for it. They inspire each other. Passion and joy are their best accessories.

As we grow as a company, it has become more and more important to explicitly define the core values from which we develop our culture, our brand, and our business strategies. These are the ten core values that we live by:

Deliver WOW Through Service
Embrace and Drive Change
Create Fun and A Little Weirdness
Be Adventurous, Creative, and Open-Minded
Pursue Growth and Learning
Build Open and Honest Relationships With Communication
Build a Positive Team and Family Spirit
Do More With Less
Be Passionate and Determined
Be Humble

WE'RE GUIDED BY 1 SIMPLE MISSION.

With every product you purchase,
TOMS will help a person in need. One for One.

Our mission statement is simple...To grow a profitable airline, where people love to fly and where people love to work. Virgin believes in making a difference. We stand for value for money, quality, innovation, fun and a sense of competitive challenge. We strive to achieve this by empowering our employees to continually deliver an unbeatable customer experience.

In Phil's work as a Registered Life Planner, there are three key questions (developed by George Kinder, www.kinderinstitute.com) he asks clients to help them get focused on what's most important to them. You may find these questions helpful in developing your own personal mission statement:

QUESTION 1: Imagine that you are financially secure, that you have enough money to take care of your needs, now and in the future. How would you live your life? Would you change anything? Let yourself go and don't hold back on your dreams. Describe a life that is complete and richly yours.

QUESTION 2: Imagine you visit the doctor and discover that you only have 5-10 years left to live. The good news is that you won't feel sick and will still be able to do everything you can know. The bad news is that you will have no notice of the moment of your death. What will you do in the time you have remaining to live? Will you change your life and how will you do it?

QUESTION 3: Imagine you visit the doctor and discover you only have one day left to live. Notice the feelings that arise as you confront your very real mortality.

Ask yourself:
o What did I miss?
o Who did I not get to be?
o What did I not get to do?

ACTION ITEM CHECKLIST

☐ Take a few blank pieces of paper and a pen and sit in a quiet place. Then, for the next ten minutes, **WRITE WHAT YOU BELIEVE YOU WERE PUT ONTO THIS EARTH TO ACHIEVE.** Don't edit, don't censor yourself, don't even write in complete sentences if you don't want to—just let it all out onto the paper. **WRITE WHAT YOU'D LIKE TO STAND FOR, WHAT GIFTS YOU'D LIKE TO GIVE TO THE WORLD, AND WHAT VALUES YOU WANT TO BE REMEMBERED FOR.** Don't write what you feel you should want, or you should do—remember, no one will see this but you! Just be honest.

☐ Now, go over what you wrote and **CRAFT THE ESSENCE OF IT INTO A PERSONAL MISSION STATEMENT.** Whenever you've achieved a victory in your business, or hit a stumbling block, this is what you will fall back on. You can keep it in your desk drawer, print it on fancy paper and frame it, even hang it on your fridge—but keep it as your touchstone for the future.

☐ And, the next time someone asks what you do at your business, also **TELL THEM WHY**—make your values an integral part of your products and services.

Meet the New
SUPER HEROES*!*

LESS IS MORE
KAREN BATCHELOR
Living Large With Less

Renaissance woman Karen Batchelor is one of the most extraordinary women we've ever met. She's a corporate attorney and high-powered lobbyist who woke up one day and decided to massively shift her life. In addition, she was the first African-American member of the Daughters of the American Revolution (DAR) and the only person we know personally who was actually the answer to a question on the TV show Jeopardy!

She stepped away from the world of power suits and expensive lunches to embark on a career as a life coach for mid-career professionals in search of significance – in addition to success – at the ripe young age of 56. With many who embark on such a path, Karen encountered a few false starts along the way, but eventually found her "true groove."

She now coaches women senior executives, career changers, dissatisfied empty nesters, and mid-life crisis experiencers on "Living Large with Less" – a unique and powerful approach that consists of shedding the encumbering – and unnecessary trappings of the "big life" to live simply, joyfully, and passionately. Her personal passion is to downsize to a 250-square foot tiny house, continue chasing down her ancestors, and embrace personal freedom and happiness beyond the clutter called "success."

Karen is extraordinary talented at helping mid-career professional women discover what's missing in their lives and then chart a course to create personal – as well as professional – satisfaction. In addition to the work she's currently doing with Living Large with Less, Karen's also the author of *Amazing Life After 50*.

Her courage and determination to define success on her own terms secures her a top spot on our list of the new Wonder Women.

You can learn more about Karen and her unique approach to fulfillment at www.livinglargewithless.com.

NOTES

2

sus·tain·a·bility, n.

1. Capable of giving support or relief to;

2. Capable of supplying with sustenance or nourishment;

3. Capable of being kept up or prolonged;

4. Capable of supporting the weight of; also: to carry or withstand a weight or pressure;

5. *The Wonder Women Way:* By creating structure and a strong legal foundation, you create something sustainable, which also encapsulates prudence, wisdom, courage, and diligence.

SUSTAINABILITY

Get Your Legal Ducks In a Row

Create your legal structure on day one. This is not a luxury. It is not something that can wait.

Aside from a brilliant product or offering, your legal foundation is the next single most important thing to get buttoned up. That is because failing to take care of this can lead to the loss of intellectual property, your brand, or even your entire business.

From our experience, when working with entrepreneurs, the majority tell us they wish they had focused on taking care of their legal foundation from the beginning. And because we are so passionate about this, we are going to give you a detailed roadmap right here so you know what legal tasks need to be addressed as soon as possible!

If you are going to go to the trouble of creating a business, why would you stop short of protecting it?

– Jessica Eaves Mathews

Going into business for yourself is all about the pursuit of a positive work/life balance—inner fulfillment and living life on your own terms. Those terms are different for everyone. Some entrepreneurs are going to be empire builders with offices that span the nation, and others are going to happily remain small business owners in their local town. Some will define success as a seven-figure enterprise, and others will define it merely as being their own boss, no matter what their income. For almost all of us, though, success can be defined as doing what you love to do, having time to be with your loved ones, and enjoying the freedom to pursue the opportunities you're passionate about.

But stop for a minute. Just doing what you love and hoping for the best is not enough to protect your entrepreneurial endeavors, you, or your family. **Success is completely dependent upon making sure you have a strong legal foundation on which to build your enterprise.** This foundation must be structured in a way that maximizes your chances for success and minimizes common risks that can undo all your hard work or even put you out of business.

So, here is your roadmap. We strongly encourage you to develop a relationship with a good business lawyer now – one who understands your business and your industry – so that you make sure you are protected every step of the way. It will give you peace of mind and free you up to focus on what you do best and love most.

STEP ONE: STARTING UP RIGHT
Choosing an Entity
and Setting it Up ASAP

You may be sighing or cringing at the very idea of discussing legal ideas—for many people it's as exciting as watching paint dry, and maybe even less so! People usually want to focus on the more "fun" tasks, like social media, branding, and promotion—but first you absolutely must get your legal house in order. Addressing the legal issues inherent in starting a business can be exciting if you view it as another step in the path to your ultimate dream! After you've protected your assets, you'll have the peace of mind that allows you the emotional and mental freedom to enjoy running and building your business.

SEPARATE AND INDEPENDENT

The first step to take to protect business is to set up a proper business entity. Setting up this entity should be your first priority. A business entity is separate and independent from your personal identity. Those two words are very important! Your goal throughout your day-to-day operations for your business should be to keep your business separate and independent from you as an individual. If your business is truly separate and independent, then your personal assets like your house, your car, or whatever it is that you cherish are generally safe from business liabilities (though there are, of course, exceptions to this rule).

BUSINESS ENTITIES

For US-based businesses, there are several types of business entities to choose from, but for a small start-up there are really only three basic choices:

LLCs : Limited Liability Companies

S-Corps : S-Corporations

C-Corps : C-Corporations
(what you think of when you think of a traditional corporation.)

If you are in another country, like Canada, the LLC form may not be available to you. Make sure you check with a reputable small business attorney in your area to give you guidance on what entity is the best for you. But don't let anyone tell you being a sole-proprietor is the right choice. In any country, it always puts your personal assets at risk!

SOLE PROPRIETORSHIP

What if you've already started your business but haven't set up an entity? Don't beat yourself up about it! Many small businesses operate as a sole proprietorship, and if you've never had any kind of entity set up, by default you are sole proprietorship. **The problem with the sole proprietorship is that you have absolutely no protection from liabilities that arise from your business activities.** That's a really big deal, obviously. That means that if someone sues you to collect on a bill – for example one incurred by your business – they can potentially access your personal property to satisfy that debt. You may lose your house, your car, or any other property in which you own equity. If you're in a community property state, creditors are also going to have access to community or marital property. As you can see, there's a big risk in operating as a sole proprietorship, and we always advise against that business structure.

PARTNERSHIP

If you have a business partner and you haven't set up a legal entity you are, by default, a partnership. Just as a sole proprietorship, if you are a partnership then you have total exposure to business liabilities for both yourself and your partners, no matter how many of you there are.

There are, obviously, costs involved in setting up an entity but they greatly outweigh the risks of having no entity in place at all.

LLCs

Luckily, business entities are easy to understand and set up! An LLC is the ideal choice for most small business owners. It's a great way to start because it gives you limited liability, just like it says. Now, it doesn't provide absolute protection from liability—it is called limited liability, after all—but you will have a lot of protection. You also enjoy certain tax benefits, including "pass through" taxation, which means that any revenue that comes into your business and the profits that result after your expenses are taxed only on your personal income tax level.

This is different from the taxation structure of a corporation, which is hit with "double taxation." In corporations, the net revenue will be taxed on the corporate level first, and then any money you pull out of that company, such as a salary or a distribution, is going to be taxed again on a personal income tax level. In other words, the IRS gets two bites out of the same apple. With an LLC, you avoid that and the IRS only gets to tax you *once*.

C-CORPORATION

There are only a few situations where a C-Corporation makes sense for the start-up business owner. For purposes of the business owners reading this book, one is if you intend to sell the business in the future, and another is if you want to attract investors. Most people who are buying a company have no interest in buying a LLC, and if you know that you're going to be raising capital at some point in the form of venture capital, angel funds, or through selling shares on the open market, then you must bite the bullet and be a C-Corp. There are some tax benefits to being a C-Corp, but for most small businesses they are not significant enough to justify the cost. You can always switch from an LLC to a C-Corp later if the need arises (but it is much harder and more expensive to switch from a C-Corp to an LLC, so if in doubt, start with an LLC). So if you are in doubt or if the above doesn't apply to you, start as an LLC.

S-CORPORATION

An S-Corp is really just a tax election (again, this only applies to US-based businesses), meaning that you tell the IRS that you want to be treated as an S-Corp. You start out as either an LLC or a corporation first. As an S-Corp, you will still be taxed as a partnership, as with the LLC, but there are significant tax savings in being an S-Corp once you reach a certain level of positive tax flow for your business. However, you won't see much significant savings in self-employment taxes until you start making at least six-figures in revenue. Your CPA can tell you for sure when you will start seeing the benefits, so definitely ask her.

The great thing about an S-Corp is that you can elect it later, so you can start out as a LLC and then make the tax selection for S-Corp once it makes sense to do so. It is important to note the downside of being an S-Corp, as well: You have to maintain "corporate formalities," which means having annual meetings and minutes and corporate resolutions for every major decision. You have to keep your record books in your place of business, and you have to be very meticulous with the paperwork, so it's a lot more work to maintain an S-Corp than a LLC. You really need to make sure you are going to benefit financially from having done it. If you don't maintain those formalities and you get challenged by the IRS, you could lose that S-Corp tax treatment and will be barred from claiming it again for the next five years. It's not something to take lightly, so talk to your CPA before you make any decisions.

So, now you've avoided one hidden legal disaster and protected your personal assets—but how do you protect your business name and thus your reputation and integrity? That involves claiming and owning the name of your company and brand.

SHOW ME THE MONEY!

Be sure to set up a separate bank account for your business entity—remember, we are keeping your business as separate from your life as possible! Do not, under any circumstances, comingle business and personal funds. Your business cannot be truly separate and independent if you're comingling funds.

If you are sued by a creditor who is trying to reach your personal assets and you've been using a business credit card or account for personal reasons or vice versa, a court might determine that there is no real distinction between you and the business, and then you could lose your limited liability protection. This is called "piercing the corporate veil"—to avoid that outcome, you must be vigilant about maintaining the distinction between your business and your life.

Google. Coca-Cola. Mary Kay. Facebook. Starbucks. Nike. What do all these things have in common? They have a trademark in place that keeps any other company from infringing on their identity and products! Yes, the second step to take to protect your business is to secure your business name and even your logo with a trademark.

Business names, offerings, product names and logos can be trademarked. If you have a unique tagline or slogan, that can be trademarked, too—for instance, Nike's "Just do it" and Burger King's "Have it your way" are both protected phrases. Finally, if you have a unique trade dress—that is, the appearance of your product or packaging—you can even trademark that! Tiffany, for instance, has trademarked the unique turquoise shade it uses for all its jewelry boxes!

IN INTERSTATE COMMERCE:

Keep in mind that you must be offering something for sale in commerce in order to qualify for a trademark. In the US, that means that you must be offering a good or service for sale across state lines, and not just in one state. If you offer goods off of a website, for example, you are "in commerce" since someone from any state can purchase from you. But to qualify for a trademark, you will need to show the date of your first sale ACROSS STATE LINES, so make sure you keep a note of that and have documentation to prove it.

There is a THREE-STEP PROCESS involved in establishing full trademark protection, and you want to begin this process as soon as possible. We walk you through that process on the next page.

3 STEPS
get your trademark !

The **FIRST STEP** is to immediately begin using the **TM** symbol after your company name, logo, or tagline. This puts the world on notice that you are claiming a trademark.

The **SECOND STEP** is to document the date on which you began using the trademark "in commerce." If there is a dispute over trademark ownership, the trademark office will look to see who put the mark into use in interstate commerce first in order to determine ownership of the mark. You must make sure that there is no way your proof of trademark date can be falsified. Dated screenshots, invoices, dated emails, dated brochures or event materials are all good examples of proof that will satisfy this requirement for the trademark office.

The **THIRD STEP** in the trademark protection process is to file for trademark registration with the United States Patent Trademark Office (USPTO—you can visit this agency's website at www.uspto.gov). You can go this alone, but it's not necessarily as simple as it seems. You may get a response back from the USPTO either rejecting your application or asking for additional documentation or information. If this happens, we strongly suggest hiring someone to help you get through the remaining steps of the process.

PROVE IT?
How to prove your date of first use

Just starting out and about to use your brand name for the first time in commerce? Print the document you will use to prove your use as soon as you begin using it (like when your website goes live and your have your first sale) and put it in an envelope, seal it really well, address it to yourself, and mail it to yourself through the U.S. mail. When you receive it, don't open it! Just file it away in case of a later dispute. Voila! The postmark will be conclusive proof of the date.

If you're planning on only selling your products or services **in state**, of course file for a state trademark through your state government—but if you have a website, you are potentially "in commerce" whether you like it or not. That means you'll also need to apply for a federal trademark, if you want to own your own brand.

Internationally, you'll have to meet many additional requirements. That process is quite complicated, and you will almost certainly need legal assistance in that situation.

STEP THREE: COPYRIGHT
Protecting Your Brilliant Ideas

If you want to keep your brilliant ideas as your own—benefitting you and your business—the third step you must take is to get a copyright! Many people think they don't have a copyright until they file for it with the government, but that's not true—actually, as soon as you create an original work, whether it's a sales video, tele-seminar, video, webinar, PowerPoint, portrait, architectural drawings, novel, lyrics—you name it—you have a copyright! It automatically attaches to your work.

However, without a registered copyright you only have limited remedies in the court. So how do you get a registered trademark? Read on!

HOW TO
get your registered copyright !

Once you've written or created your original piece of work, THE FIRST STEP is to start marking it with the "circle c" and your name: for instance, *"©2013 Leverage-a-Lawyer LLC. All rights reserved."* This puts the world on notice that the material is yours and cannot be impermissibly copied without legal consequences.

The SECOND STEP is to either hire a lawyer like one at Leverage Legal Group or if you are inclined to do it yourself, visit www.copyright.gov and fill out the copyright application. You will have to attach a copy of the item you want protected (a digital version, if filing online), and pay the filing fee.

THIRD STEP, get ready to wait! It can take up to a year to get notification of your registered copyright, but once you apply you have a provisional protection, just like with the trademark, so you just want to get your application in as soon as possible.

TO OWN OR NOT TO OWN: You will need to think about whether you want to own your intellectual property as an individual (which then it would make it a personal asset) or if you want your company to own it.

Some people set up a holding company to hold the assets they use in their business, and then set up a separate operating company to keep the operations separate from business assets. That might sound a little complicated, but it just means that if you get sued for your operations your assets are not housed in the same entities so they are not subject to being sold off to satisfy a judgment.

If you want to sell your business in the future, you should have your entity own your intellectual property, your copyright, and your trademark, because those are assets and anyone buying your business in the future would want those included in the deal.

MY DESIGNER OWNS WHAT??

If you hire a third party to help you create work product for your business, whether it's a copywriter, a virtual assistant, even a web designer, the common law rule is that the independent contractor actually owns the copyright to that work! Now, the rules have some exceptions that get a little complicated, but a good rule of thumb is to assume that your contractor or service provider might own the copyright in the work they are doing for you.

To prevent that, you must have the person sign a contract transferring their ownership rights to you and your business. Otherwise he or she can use that content in any way she wants, including selling it to a competitor or distributing as his or her own work product. In fact, have your employees sign the same agreement, just to make sure you are as protected as you can be. This contract is called a "work for hire" agreement.

We don't recommend drafting this on your own. Instead, ask your lawyer for one or download the "work for hire" agreement template from the Leverage-a-Lawyer website (look under the contract templates). You can either use this separately or, better yet, make it part of your Non-Disclosure Agreement, which you also should be using with everyone who works in your business. What's that? It's the fourth step you need to take to protect your business! Read on!

While you're waiting for approval of that copyright, continue to use the © symbol and the year, as well as the holder of the copyright (either you or your business). Add the words "All rights reserved" and you have a solid copyright statement.

The fourth step to take to protect your business is to have every employee and every single contractor who works for you sign a Non-Disclosure Agreement (NDA). An NDA is absolutely critical to protecting your ideas and your proprietary information. Think of it as a tripod: The way you protect your intellectual property and your ideas and your assets is to have a trademark as one leg of the tripod, your copyright as the other, and your Non-Disclosure Agreement as your third. **You're not fully protected unless you have all three in place!** We like to call it a Super Power Trifecta!

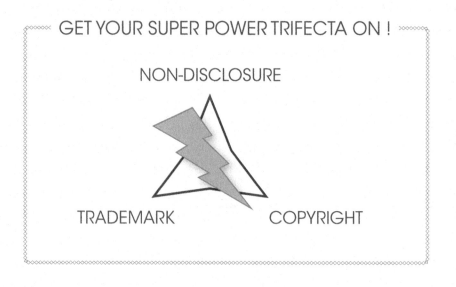

GET YOUR SUPER POWER TRIFECTA ON !

NON-DISCLOSURE

TRADEMARK   COPYRIGHT

The NDA basically says that the person working for you cannot disclose, share or distribute in any way the confidential and proprietary information that they learn as a result of working with you. That's going to protect your email list, your client names, your client information, any kind of business plans for the future, products that are in development, financial information, and everything else pertaining to your business. You are in essence letting them "behind the curtain" of your business.

INSIDER TIP

Never let anyone behind the curtain of your business without first making them sign one of these agreements. If they balk or won't sign it, do not hire them.

Note: Potential investors likely won't sign an NDA, because they see so many deals and don't want to be limited as to what they can invest in. So there are some roles that will not be covered by an NDA. But anyone who is working for you absolutely must sign one.

Your web designer is in charge of making your website polished and professional and representative of your business's unique image. But you do have one crucial responsibility with your website that the designer is not in charge of. **The fifth step to take to protect your business is to include proper documentation and disclaimers on your website.**

There are people who surf the web who are litigious and are looking for "deep pockets"—that is, they're looking for someone to sue! Having the proper documentation on your website can deter some of this dangerous behavior. The three most important documents to include are the Terms of Use Agreement, a Privacy Policy, and a Terms of Sale. All three of these will greatly help minimize trouble from people using, visiting, and accessing your website.

TERMS OF USE AGREEMENT

A Terms of Use Agreement is actually an enforceable contract. It sits on your website under the "Terms of Use" or "Terms of Service" tab. On many websites it sits at the very bottom in small print, but it needs to be a page people can easily access. This agreement spells out in detail the terms required—basically, the conditions upon which someone is going to use your website. If your site contains copyrighted content, offers any kind of advice, or sells products or services, a Terms of Use Agreement is a must. What needs to be in it depends on your business.

If you have any type of fiduciary relationship with a client, you need to have that kind of disclaimer in your Terms of Use. If you have a blog or a site that allows for social interaction, as in an interactive forum, you have to have a Terms of Use that governs those activities and reserves your right to exclude people from your website without liability.

Jessica has a golf clothing line called Grace & Game, clothing for women inspired by golf and the country club lifestyle. Since she sells clothing on her website, she needs a Terms of Use Agreement that governs the terms under which customers will actually purchase items from her website. For instance, it might say something like, "The colors that are on your screen may not be the exact color of the item you receive, and we are not responsible for this disparity." Or, she might need a disclaimer reading that she doesn't guarantee that she will always have the size or inventory of a particular item.

Service based businesses are a little different. For example, on Jessica's law firm website, which offers professional services, the Terms of Use includes a statement that no attorney-client relationship is formed by the mere use of the website or by the mere act of sending an email or by using the contact form on the website. If you have any type of fiduciary relationship with a client, you need to have that kind of disclaimer in your Terms of Use.

♥ No matter what your business is, you need to give some thought to what you might be exposed to liability-wise and then add those to the Terms of Use Agreement. Retaining a good lawyer who knows how to draft a Terms of Use for your business is a really good idea and, as an alternative, we offer a great template on Leverage-a-Lawyer. It's very broad and covers a lot of different things, so it's kind of catchall. If you don't have a big legal budget and you can't hire someone to customize it for you, buy a Terms of Use template and then hire a lawyer for an hour or two of their time to just review and revise it. It's going to cost you a lot less money than having a lawyer draft it from the beginning. - *Jessica*

Visit www.leverage-a-lawyer.com

PRIVACY POLICY

The second thing you need clearly posted on your website is a Privacy Policy. This is particularly important if you have any kind of forms on your website that collect personal data, such as email addresses or other personally identifying information, from visitors. If you have an opt-in box, you also need to post an abbreviated policy right below it, saying that you never share information with third parties. That should be a live link that people can click that will take them down to the detailed Privacy Policy, which should sit right next to your Terms of Use tab on the bottom of your website.

Privacy policies are essential not only to protect you, but also to build trust with your customers and clients. We've all seen the privacy faux pas that have happened with Facebook in the last couple of years—people care passionately about their privacy, and they do not take it lightly when you use their personal information in an unauthorized way or a way they didn't expect. In order to build trust, which we all know is so critical in today's world of relationship marketing, you must have a clear policy about how you are going to use the information you gather. Then make sure you live by it! Breaking trust can cost you clients and your reputation.

TERMS OF SALE

The final important disclaimer to include on your website is Terms of Sale or Terms and Conditions. Terms of Sale is an enforceable contract that governs the sale of any goods or services via a shopping cart on your site. Many shopping carts and merchant accounts provide a boilerplate contract with your cart, but you should never rely on that. You need to be sure that the terms contained in that agreement are customized for your business and track your policies (like when to give refunds). Don't overlook this, because if someone wants to get a refund or complain about a good or service they purchased from you, the Terms of Sale will be what govern the relationship. NOTE: Terms of Use govern access to and use of your website, not monetary transactions. To have the most protection, you need both a Terms of Use and Terms of Sale.

Just like with protecting your ideas, the Terms of Use, Privacy Policy and Terms of Sale are like a three legged stool—you aren't protected without all three.

TERMS OF USE AGREEMENT

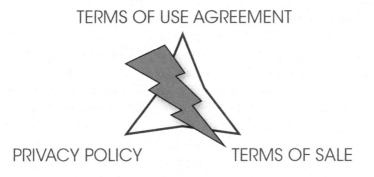

PRIVACY POLICY   TERMS OF SALE

These three documents are easy to include on your website and will save you a lot of hassle—after all, you want to focus on serving customers and providing the best business possible, not fending off lawsuits!

FUN
FACTOID

"CLICK WRAP AGREEMENT"

When Microsoft and the other early software companies started selling software to the public, they came up with a way to make sure the Terms of Sale that they wanted to govern each sale was enforceable against the customer. The solution they came up with was to wrap the box in plastic shrink wrap and print the contract on a label that was then affixed to the plastic wrap. It specifically said that if you opened the plastic wrapping to open the box, you were agreeing to the terms of the sales agreement. This became known as a "Shrink Wrap Agreement."

When the internet came into being and companies started selling software downloads online, they needed the equivalent way to make sure there was an agreement that governed that transaction. What resulted was a check box that the customer must read and then agree to by checking the box before the transaction can be completed. This is known now as a "Click Wrap Agreement."

These agreements have been found by courts to be enforceable and you need one on your cart (ideally, make your client or customer click to agree to the terms before the sale is completed).

Despite the First Amendment, free speech has its limits. You can't yell fire in a crowded theater, and you can't email someone who doesn't agree to be emailed! The sixth step to protect your business is knowing and following the federal rules governing email and consumer-protection disclosures.

THE FEDERAL CAN-SPAM ACT:

If you send out email communications to your customers or clients, you have no choice: you absolutely must adhere to the federal Can-Spam Act, or you can find yourself being prosecuted and fined heavily for being a spammer. This is no small thing! Jessica had a client who regularly marketed his business via email almost go out of business because he was embroiled in litigation with the U.S. Attorney's office out of New York for a violation of the Can-Spam Act.

So now that we've scared you, how do you avoid this problem? **Basically, you just need to have clear authorization to contact someone via email.** The way to do that is to only add someone to your email list who has given you explicit permission to do so, and the best way to do that is with an opt-in box, where people can choose whether they want to opt in or not.

We've seen some dialogue about this on Facebook recently. If someone friends you on Facebook, do not go in and find their email address and their info and add them to your list. So many people are starting to do this—but it's illegal! It's a violation of a federal statute, and there are people who are getting angry enough about it that they might report you. There is a per violation fine associated with this act, so if you have a decent-sized list you can get fined for anyone who's on that list that you didn't have authorization to send an email to. It can add up very, very quickly, so just don't do it. Let people opt in, and let them also opt out very easily. Make sure they can find a way to opt out and that it happens instantaneously. Obviously, the best way to do this is to have a service manage it for you, such as 1ShoppingCart, iContact, Mail Chimp or Constant Contact, or the like because those programs receive the unsubscribe request and keep, basically, a "do not contact" list for you.

FTC DISCLOSURES REGARDING CLIENT TESTIMONIALS:

Your website must also follow the Federal Trade Commission (FTC) rules. In December, 2009, the FTC began to enforce revisions to the guidance it gives to advertisers – and we are all advertisers if we're advertising anything for sale. If you put testimonials on your website from former or current clients or customers, then you're subject to FTC guidelines and must disclose your connection to those who are praising your products, as well as disclaiming that the results in the testimonial are not typical. In fact, not only must you say clearly that the results are not typical, you must be ready to document and prove what IS typical. This last rule hasn't been tested much yet, but be aware it exists and keep good records of the kinds of results your customers are getting so you can respond if the FTC ever challenges you.

Drafting these disclaimers can be a little daunting, because the FTC has just instituted this rule and has not given a lot of guidance, Leverage-a-Lawyer.com has instructional audio that you can use to get some help. As time goes on the exact requirements of the rules will become more clear, because people are going to get busted and we're going to get more clarity from the FTC on what it means to be in compliance with these rules. The very best thing to do is to just clearly state that you cannot make any guarantees about your product or services. This is best placed in the Terms of Use as well as under the actual testimonials. Also include it in your email communications or in social media if you are using testimonials there.

FTC DISCLOSURES REGARDING AFFILIATE RELATIONSHIPS:

Finally, you are required by FTC rules to disclose affiliate relationships (that is, a relationship in which the recommender gets paid by the product or service provider to make the positive recommendation). Many businesspeople use affiliate relationships in order to spread the word about our products and services, but the FTC is really cracking down on this because they don't want the public to be misled.

How could an affiliate relationship mislead a customer? It's simple. When someone raves about a company, or is in a position of authority or admiration and makes a recommendation, it carries weight—but if that person is getting paid to tout the product or service, that might affect the recommendation's credibility.

So, the FTC is saying you need to disclose paid recommendations and affiliate relationships. If you use or are involved in an affiliate relationship, make sure this information is clearly posted—you don't want there to be any confusion about it. You can use boilerplate language, such as, "In some instances I will make a recommendation for which I am compensated; however, I will never make a recommendation for something that I don't believe in or haven't personally experienced. You can trust my recommendations, but know that in some cases I will get some type of remuneration for having made that recommendation."

Err on the side of being safe with affiliate and testimonial disclosures, because again, the business community is not exactly sure yet how it's all going to come out with the FTC's enforcement.

STEP SEVEN:
RELATIONSHIP INSURANCE
The Necessity of Contracts

The seventh *(but not final – there is more to do, but these seven steps will get you a solid start!)* step to take to protect your business is to have a contract that governs each and every relationship within your business. If you're hiring vendors, have a Retainer Agreement with that vendor. Make sure that the contract governs the price, payment, or fee of the relationship, the time period the relationship covers, and very specifically what the parties are agreeing to do for each other. Have all of this information clearly written out.

If you're bringing on clients, have them sign a detailed Client Agreement. This agreement is a great communication tool, and unfortunately it's an area that so many entrepreneurs skip—they may think it seems like overkill or that a client will be offended by the suggestion that you need a signed contract to trust them. **However, true professionals understand the need for good contracts, and they're not going to give you a hard time about it.** The beauty of a Client Agreement is that by going through the process of negotiating the agreement you're going to set out really clear expectations for each party, so that everyone knows the scope of their role and their exact responsibilities; it also governs what happens in the event of a dispute, which is very important.

Contracts make some people uncomfortable—they might become sensitive or insulted, just like you perhaps would be if someone presented you with a pre-nup before you got married. If you're afraid of offending someone, try to think of it in a different way—how someone responds to your request that the relationship be governed by a well-crafted contract is a test for the relationship, because, as we said before, a true professional is going to understand why it's important. It protects them, too. If someone balks at it or gets offended, that's a huge red flag, and we encourage you to run away from someone like that. It's going to save you a huge amount of heartache and money on the backend.

AS NIKE SAYS...JUST DO IT!

Now we've gone through the seven steps you must take to protect your business—and as you can see, they're all easily done. If you've already started your business, don't panic—it's not too late to take any of these steps! Take a deep breath and tackle a few of these issues at a time. File for your entity, take steps to copyright and trademark your work and business name, make sure you have strong, solid contracts with your employees, staff, vendors and clients, use disclaimers liberally, and be careful who you email! A strong legal foundation is the cornerstone of having a successful business and a necessity for protecting your assets and assuring your peace of mind.

Tending to the legal foundation of your business is profound. It is stepping into and embracing your power. It is honoring yourself and your hard work. It is ensuring your future success. It is making a bold statement to the world that you are to be taken seriously. That, my friends, is business brilliant.

- Jessica Eaves Mathews

ACTION ITEM CHECKLIST

☐ Figure out which entity you are and set it up in the next week.

☐ Get a federal tax ID number for your business (called an EIN or FEIN) *(http://www.irs.gov)*.

☐ Open a separate bank account for your business (you will need your EIN for this, as well as your Certificate of Formation or Articles of Incorporation from the state).

When working on the tasks below, we highly suggest retaining the services of a good lawyer (like Jessica Eaves Mathews.) They will be able to guide you through the entire process and answer any questions you may have.

☐ Start the process of securing a State, Federal, or International Trademark for your business.

☐ Secure registered copyrights (a good copyright lawyer will be able to help you determine what needs protection).

☐ Start using a Non-Disclosure Agreement with every single person you "let behind the curtain" in your business.

☐ Write your Privacy Policy, Terms of Use, and Terms of Sale for your website based on your needs and implement them.

☐ Read the Federal Can-Spam Act and FTC rules and make sure you are in compliance. If not, talk to a good internet lawyer (like Jessica!) about how to get in compliance and stay there.

☐ Have your lawyer draft a customized Vendor or Independent Contractor Retainer Agreement and Client Agreement (or the like, depending on your business), and start using them with every single relationship in your business.

NOTES

in·teg·ri·ty, n.

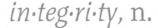

1. Steadfast adherence to a strict moral or ethical code;

2. The state of being unimpaired; soundness;

3. The quality or condition of being whole or undivided; completeness;

4. Incorruptible;

5. *The Wonder Women Way*: doing not just what is authentic, but what is right - doing no harm and leaving the world a better place.

INTEGRITY

Doing Good Beyond the Bottom Line

"It's Not Just Business...It's Personal."

Forget what you learned from the Godfather ("go to the mattresses!") or Donald Trump. The biggest mistake we made as an economy in the past few decades was to forget that business is always personal...and it should be. Unfortunately, the majority of workers in corporate America wake up every business day, put on a suit of armor before leaving the house, and exist throughout the work day only showing the world the small sliver of themselves visible through their armor's visor to their bosses, co-workers, customers, and clients. When they get home, they take off that suit of armor and become their "real" selves again.

The term 'success' should include the values of wellbeing, wisdom and kindness. Go-getters, I hope, will become 'go-givers.'

– Arianna Huffington

We firmly believe that living and working this way is a colossal waste of potential and opportunity and challenge you to approach business with greater authenticity and transparency. Don't be afraid to let who you really are shine through! We don't mean wear your heart on your sleeve and cry at McDonald's commercials (we certainly never do... ahem...). What we mean is that what you do matters. Be generous and help others succeed.

The Founder of Yum! Brand Foods, David Novak said, "take people with you. It is the only way to make big things happen. And it will impact not only you and your team, but your family, their families, your community and even the world." John Mackey, the CEO of Whole Foods, while attending Arianna Huffington's first Third Metric event in June 2013 talked about the need for... wait for it...love. These are his words:

"We can't solve the problems at the consciousness we're currently at. We need our leaders to release love. Love is in the closet. And we all know women on average have a much higher emotional, spiritual and social intelligence than men do. Men's metaphors for corporations are primarily war metaphors, sports metaphors, and Darwinian metaphors— survival of the fittest. Those are antithetical to having love in the culture. So, if love is going to come out of the corporate closet, it's going to have to be women who release it."

See? You are what we need. YOU. You bring the very things that are missing from business today. And when people like the CEO of Whole Foods and *Forbes* magazine start to acknowledge this truth, it is huge validation of what we have been talking about since we started writing this book. So, given that you are what the world needs, the biggest mistake you could make would be to leave your humanity at the door.

WHAT YOU
DO MATTERS

+

BE GENEROUS

+

HELP OTHERS
SUCCEED

Bring your humanity, your empathy, your compassion, your passion, your sense of humor and your hopes and dreams to work every day and let them infuse your business. As great leaders like Tony Hsieh of Zappos, Blake Mycoskie of Toms Shoes and Jessica Jackley of Kiva.org will tell you – making it personal is what will make your business great. It will make you a ton of money, and it will make you a leader.

Meet the New SUPER HEROES!

BEYOND THE BOTTOM LINE: Instead of talking at you about why bringing your integrity and humanity to your business is important, we felt that it would be much more profound to show you some examples of business owners who are doing that very thing, and who are wildly successful not in spite of this, but BECAUSE of this. For inspiration, read on, young super heroes!

STORIES OF DIGNITY

JESSICA JACKLEY, Kiva.org

Jessica Jackley is the co-founder of Kiva.org, the world's first peer-to-peer online microlending website (she co-founded it with her then husband, Matt Flannery). Kiva.org was launched in 2004 and by 2006, it was named as one of the top ideas of the year by the *New York Times Magazine*. For those who haven't heard of it yet, Kiva.org enables individuals to lend as little as $25 to actual entrepreneurs in developing countries and in the U.S. The point is to enable entrepreneurs to get access to capital to help them start or expand a business.

When asked about why and how Kiva came about, she said: "The things I really care about are people. The numbers are really interesting, but their not really what makes my heart sing. They aren't what I think is the end game to change...What changes the world is when people think of each other differently."

What started Jessica on the road to Kiva was a high school trip to Haiti, where she experienced and witnessed people living in poverty for the first time. At home, she was a popular high school senior who worried about things like prom, while the people she met in Haiti spent their whole days working just so they could eat. It changed things for her.

After getting married and moving to California, Jessica got a job at Stanford as an assistant. She didn't have to do the course work, but got to attend lectures there, and she spent three years getting to do that. One of the people she heard speak was Dr. Muhammad Yunus at Stanford. He told his story about the work he was doing internationally and one thing stood out for her: He said that he would meet with people in developing countries, learn about their stories and lives, and he would reach in his pocket and lend $24 and change the whole village.

It was a lightening bolt. This approach made sense to her head and her heart. Dr. Yunus talked about the people he helped with respect and dignity. Jessica decided she wanted to go do something like he did. So a few months later, she went to East Africa with a group that gave out $100 grants and went to a new village every 2-3 days and interviewed entrepreneurs who received these $100 loans. Through it, she learned their stories – not stories of pain, death and hopelessness like we see on TV – were of dignity and hope. Stories of triumph, effort and people doing extraordinary things. Beautiful, hopeful and intriguing stories.

Jessica and her husband started sharing those stories, and before long, friends and family wanted to help these people by lending them small amounts of money (not donating). And lending was what they needed – not a handout. These were business people. And Kiva.org was born. They did $500k in loans that first year, and the following year they did $14M. All in little $25 increments.

Since that time, Kiva has been particularly instrumental in supporting female entrepreneurship in developing countries. In 2012, close to 82% of their borrowers were women in 220 countries around the world. Kiva has been one of the fastest-growing social benefit websites in history, and today facilitates over $1.5M dollars each week from lenders to entrepreneurs in those 220 countries.

HONEST GOODNESS

JESSICA ALBA
The Honest Company, *in her own words:*

"Becoming a mom has been the most profound, life-changing experience and I'll never look at the world the same. Having a child made me so much more aware of the dangers and risks all around my new baby; it seemed like overnight an instinct to protect kicked in.

For decades, parents have been taking precautions to reduce dangers around their children by using car seats, child gates, outlet covers and more. But today there are many invisible risks that most parents aren't aware of – risks from everyday products we buy for our homes and children.

When I was pregnant with my daughter, Honor, I read Christopher Gavigan's book, Healthy Child Healthy World: Creating a Cleaner, Greener, Safer Home. This book served as my handbook on toxic chemicals in products and their link to illnesses. I learned that our current chemical regulatory system is doing an abysmal job of protecting us, the consumers. Simply put, manufacturers are allowed to use questionable, untested, toxic chemicals in everyday consumer products like baby shampoo, diapers and household cleaners.

As a lot of new parents do, I spent hours and hours researching products for my baby. Then I spent more time jumping from site to site buying products online or running around from one store to another trying to find them. I'd shell out way more money for the products in brown packaging and pictures of nature only to get home and find out the brown diapers I just bought still had ingredients in them I was trying to avoid. And the few products that were actually safer never seemed to work as well as I needed. My dishes didn't get clean. The conditioner wouldn't detangle my daughter's hair and those diapers kept leaking. I was utterly frustrated, and sick and tired of compromising.

I thought, "Wouldn't it be great if there was one company I could get all my daily essentials from – from diapers to cleaning to bath time – and I could trust that they would be safe, eco-friendly, affordable, and effective, as well as designed beautifully and delivered to my doorstep?" (I know I'm a dreamer.) What a relief it would be for me, and many parents, to have this kind of resource! I wanted and desperately needed this kind of company – so I decided to create it.

But, having a dream is the easy part. Making it happen is a whole different story. Turning any business idea into reality is hard, so I enlisted the help of experts:

• Christopher Gavigan, my co-founder and Chief Products Officer, is a nationally recognized environmental health leader, author of the aforementioned book, former Executive Director and CEO of the national non-profit of the same name, and Chief Advisor to the Green Product Innovation Institute.

• Brian Lee, eCommerce innovator, Founder of ShoeDazzle, Co-Founder of LegalZoom, and former attorney, is our CEO.

• Sean Kane, eCommerce veteran, former PriceGrabber.com executive, and expert in business operations and development, is our COO.

When I shared my idea with them, they each personally imagined how they could participate and add their expertise. And everyone agreed there was an important market niche to fill. But ultimately, being parents themselves, they all wanted this kind of company to exist for their own families, too.

So, we put our heads together and started dreaming. We dreamt up the core philosophies a brand should reach for, the culture we hoped to foster, the service that every parent needed, but didn't know they wanted yet. We sampled an expansive range of products currently available and connected with the best formulation experts and market veterans to see how we could improve on what existed. We looked into all the different options for packaging -- materials, shapes, sizes, colors – and now I know more minutiae about packaging and labels than I ever could have imagined. This is what the beginning stage of being an entrepreneur is about – exhausting all your resources, pivoting as the plan evolves and feedback rolls in, and devising solutions you believe should exist in the world.

And, with four cooks in the kitchen, we've had our fair share of respectful disagreements. For example, some people on the team weren't big fans of the idea for transparent bottles, but as a mom I felt it was important to see how much product was left in the bottle (no more running out unexpectedly mid-way through bath time). I also loved the idea of having packaging that embodied our Honest Company ethos of being transparent as a business.

After identifying exactly what we wanted to make, we carefully selected premier manufacturing partners with pristine safety records, who not only had the capabilities to meticulously craft the exceptional products we wanted, but also shared our vision of progress and creating a better world. We found our operations team and our fulfillment and shipping team to manage our inventory. We also needed a technology team that could craft a robust and stable software platform to elegantly manage our web presence, customer service interface, logistics and orders – all with the idea that it could expand and evolve over time depending on our business development. And, of course we wanted a world-class customer service team that could manage orders, have a patient ear and helpful voice.

Together, we have created The Honest Company – a monthly service that delivers customized bundles of non- toxic, eco-friendly, adorable products directly to your front door. We launched on January 17th with a product line that parents across country chose based on what they use everyday: diapers, wipes, baby bath and skin care and home cleaning products.

What will that business look like? I don't know exactly – but again, we are dreamers. I do know that the core values, passion and principles we share at Honest.com lay a strong foundation of good intentions to help "change the world." How will we turn our genuine intentions and strong beliefs that our children deserve better into a business and cultural revolution? Ask me again in ten years and hopefully I can give you the road map.

One of my favorite historical figures is Eleanor Roosevelt and her tenacity has always been an inspiration to me. She said, "You must do the thing you think you cannot do." I'm living that. People told me I couldn't start a business like this. They told me I couldn't set the bar so high. They told me I couldn't do everything I was proposing to. At first I thought maybe they were right. Not anymore.

With Honest.com, we are going to do things people think cannot be done. And we know a key to that will be honestly engaging our customers – parents – as part of this journey. It just makes sense that a brand made for families, should really listen to families. But, it goes beyond that, too. At the end of the day, we believe that together, we can make things better. Whether that's diapers, business, raising a family, homes, cleaners, connecting, bath-time, or whatever – we all have to collectively work to make this world a better place. An honest company might just be the right place to start."

Reprinted from Jessica's blog on Huffingtonpost.com
http://www.huffingtonpost.com/jessica-alba/the-honest-company_b_1300436.html

IT'S PRETTY BLACK AND WHITE

KRIS WITTENBERG
Be Good To People® & Say No More! Promotions

Sometimes, you don't plan to start a movement...instead, the movement finds you.

During the turbulent economic downturn of recent times, many of us have found ourselves wondering how it all happened. How did so many people do so many wrong things to their fellow humans? These things have led to so much distress for our neighbors, for our country and, ultimately, for our world. Even aside from economics, this is a pretty crazy world we inhabit.

They say it is often during times like these that heroes are born. And, so, it was in this environment that Be Good To People was founded. On an ordinary day, where one act of rudeness had the potential to ruin a day...entrepreneur Kris Wittenberg pondered - why can't people just be good to people?

So, in her office, where during her "day job" she has led **SayNoMore! Promotions** for the last 14 years, she began a new business built on a noble concept – Be Good To People.®

Now, **BGTP** is becoming a movement across the globe. A message of simplicity has spread to countries from the US to Canada, from France to Denmark, from Great Britain to Australia.

MISSION: *5% of Be Good to People's revenues go toward recognizing and rewarding people who are Being Good to People all over the world.*

COMPANY OVERVIEW:
It's performing simple acts of kindness, and recognizing others for their "Good."
It's a renewed feeling of hope, relief from today's negative news.
It's joy in simple things. Returning to basic, core values.
It's communicating a shared belief, like-minded people spreading a positive message.
It's a movement.
Changing the world, one person, one kind act, at a time.
The idea is simple.
It's black and white.

And guess what **BGTP** sells? Black and white t-shirts, mugs, water bottles, bags and other fun things with the words "Be Good to People" on them. Clever, right? All the products are eco-friendly and socially conscious, and the message is meant for all to share and spread. It's definitely an idea whose time has come.

For this, Kris definitely wins a spot on our colorful New Super Heroes list.

A NEW MARKETING MODEL BASED ON INTEGRITY, VALUES AND SERVICE

LISA MANYON
Write On ~ Creative Writing Services, LLC

Lisa Manyon – also known as the Superhero "The Purple Pen" – predicted the shifts we're seeing in marketing today when she penned a chapter in a book about emerging trends in marketing in 2009. She noted that many of the standard marketing techniques, especially in the copywriting arena, were antiquated and not as effective as they once were. The list included hyped-up claims, overly "sales-y" spiels, hard-sell tactics, broad-based messages, scare tactics, stretching the truth, false claims of scarcity, over-dramatizing pain and problems and more. All tactics she had seen failing and that consumers, especially women, were turned off by.

Even then she felt a collaborative shift in marketing and business. She was teaching her clients to market in a different way – a way that challenged the norm. She hadn't yet named her marketing model yet she instinctively knew it was a much better way to connect with people.

Several years later, her predictions hold true. There's a shift from competition to collaboration. This shift also requires a different approach to marketing. It requires creating marketing messages with integrity. In 2012 Manyon graced the cover of Aspire Magazine and shared her philosophies in an article she wrote called "Find Your Voice: The New Marketing Model for Success." She also named the formula she'd been teaching to help people market with integrity.

Her philosophies have since sent ripples of excitement and relief through the marketing arena, prompting requests for interviews. Her fresh approach has garnered media attention including an interview in *Inc.* magazine, radio appearances and more.

Manyon maintains that many of the techniques being taught and being used in marketing and copywriting no longer apply (they just aren't working like they once did).

In particular, Manyon challenges the age-old industry adage that "Copy is King."

Manyon says, "I've found that copy is actually QUEEN and strategy is KING and together they are the key to creating strong and effective results. Even the best copy in the world won't work if you don't have a strategy in place. Think of strategy as masculine energy and copy as feminine energy – both are vital but if they are not working together it's a struggle."

She takes her philosophies a step further. "I've also found that the traditional copywriting formula of "Problem. Agitate. Solve." isn't resonating with women. Women are looking for solutions to their challenges. What's really working is the new copywriting formula of "Challenge. Solution. Invitation.™"

In the traditional formula we're taught to highlight the issue, we're told to agitate that issue to focus on the pain points and then we solve the problem.

Manyon believes people are in enough pain. We don't need to be agitated to make a decision. In fact, especially for women, when someone acknowledges our challenges (and really understands where we're coming from), provides a helpful solution and extends a friendly invitation, we're more likely to take action. Nothing truly flows when it comes from a place of pain and fear…

The new marketing model for success comes from a place of integrity, values and service first. Anything else is transparent – and not in a good way.

Here's how you can create marketing messages with integrity using Lisa Manyon's new marketing model for success and the Challenge. Solution. Invitation.™ formula.

1) Challenge: Know your ideal clients have challenges. Acknowledge them. Understand them. Don't dwell on them or try to "agitate" or exaggerate the situation.

2) Solution: Offer a genuine solution to eliminate or alleviate the challenge. Come from a place of service first. Build relationships with your solution.

3) Invitation: Avoid hard sell tactics at all cost. Instead extend a friendly invitation to take the next step and move towards the solution. This is also considered your "call to action". It's extended in a way that builds relationships and treats people as people, not numbers.

With all of the information coming our way we have to be discerning about the messages we receive and create. It goes both ways. We receive faxes, e-mails, telephone calls, cell phone calls, instant messages, text messages, QR codes, blog posts, social media updates and more. There's permission marketing techniques, outrageous business growth philosophies that tout being aligned with your customers, qualifying prospects, the need for a website and comprehensive marketing plan and the list goes on. It's time for a change and Lisa Manyon's new marketing model for success teaches us how to create marketing messages with integrity. Marketing is truly about building relationships.

Lisa Manyon is "The Business Marketing Architect," a content and copywriting strategist for mission-driven entrepreneurs. She is the creator of the new marketing model for success as featured in *Inc.* magazine. She teaches a relationship based approach to marketing with integrity. Her "Challenge. Solution. Invitation.™" formula is changing the way we market forever. Owner of Write On ~ Creative Writing Services, LLC, Lisa is an award winning author and blogger. She's the recipient of the Charles Schwab Financial Literacy Award in The Hot Mommas Competition and is featured in the world's largest digital library of role models & mentors for women and girls.

Lisa offers free marketing resources on her award winning blog
www.writeoncreative.com/blog

INSIDER TIP

From The Purple Pen, Lisa Manyon:

"A FUNNY THING HAPPENS WHEN YOU DON'T MARKET YOUR BUSINESS…NOTHING"

5 Ways to Create Marketing Messages with Integrity
1.   Be uniquely different
2.   Work with people you want to work with
3.   Acknowledge the challenges of your clients
4.   Offer a real solution
5.   Extend a friendly invitation to take the next step

"*THE PURPLE PEN,*" Lisa Manyon, as seen through the eyes of artist Ted Helard.

A VISIONARY GO-GIVER

ARIANNA HUFFINGTON
Huffingtonpost.com

If you haven't heard of the world's first online newspaper Huffingtonpost.com, you have been living under a rock. Its founder, Arianna Huffington, has had a hand in not one but two major cultural revolutions, and she has a solid place on our list of the New Super Heroes. The first revolution was the way news was delivered. After launching Huffingtonpost.com, *Forbes* magazine ranks her among the world's most powerful women. Not only did she create a new genre for news in 2005, but she later sold it to AOL for no less than $315 million while remaining editor-in-chief.

After living decades in a business world that "men created" as she calls it, Arianna has had enough and is leading a quiet but powerful movement she has named the Third Metric. "The current model of success, in which we drive ourselves into the ground, and in which working to the point of exhaustion and burnout is a badge of honor, was created by men," says Huffington. "It's a model of success that's not working for women, and it's not working for men, either. Our workplaces are fueled by sleep deprivation." This was a quote she gave the *Telegraph* in London as she arrived in town for the second go of her new conference The Third Metric: Redefining Success Beyond Money and Power.

Her mission is to change the mindset in the workplace and move us away from what she calls the "macho culture of stress." She says, "We're constantly being pulled away from our real priorities by work and technology and what we think we need to do in order to succeed. It's very easy to lose sight of what truly matters."

Arianna believes women are central to this mission and will be its leaders in and out of the boardroom.

"The first revolution was women getting the vote, the second was getting an equal place at every level of society...The third revolution is changing the world that men have designed. It's not sustainable. Sustainability is not just about the environment, it's personal sustainability...Ironically, when we succeed at making these changes, not only are we going to have a lot of grateful men because they are paying too heavy a price, but we're going to have a lot more women at the top. Many women currently leave the workplace because they don't want to pay the price."

Arianna wasn't always an advocate of this new way of thinking. In fact, the Third Metric was the result of a wake up call she received when she fainted from exhaustion at her desk at Huffingtonpost and hit her head on her desk, breaking her cheekbone.

"When I look back, it really was an incredible gift because who knows what would have happened to me if I had not course-corrected and learnt to prioritize sleep? It also sensitized me to what was happening all around me in the workplace – heart attacks, high blood pressure, diabetes."

This once dedicated workaholic now says that having employees who work long hours is a bad thing. "Now, I always interrupt people when they praise an employee for working 24/7. I say, 'Well, this is very unfortunate. If they are working 24/7, then they can't be any good. Because nobody can be any good working 24/7.'"

She blames this workaholic mindset on men, who need to compete to the extreme with each other, resulting in unsustainable work habits. "We have a lot of leaders with high IQs in politics, business and the media making terrible decisions. This is not because they are not smart, but because they are disconnected from their own wisdom and best judgment. They are too stressed and tired."

So how did Arianna put this epiphany into action in her own life and business? First, she focused on self-care. She worked on getting more sleep, and getting more exercise, including yoga. She started meditating. But she didn't stop there. She went on a mission to help her 850 employees also. She even installed beds and sleep pods in the New York offices of The Huffington Post. Then, she set up weekly meditation and yoga classes for employees. Finally, she instructed everyone that they were neither expected nor required to respond to emails that were sent out after hours. That could wait until the next business day.

"We have a phrase at The Huffington Post: Unplug and recharge. In just the same way we must plug in our devices to recharge them, we need to unplug ourselves in order to recharge."

With the Third Metric, she is now working to revolutionize all work environments, so that all go-getters can eventually become healthy, happy, balanced go-givers.

ANGELIQUE REWERS
The Corporate Agent & Bon Mot Communications

What do you do when you're a rapidly-rising corporate communications executive for a Fortune 125 company positioned to become its youngest director at the ripe old age of 26? If you're Angelique Rewers, CEO and Founder of both The Corporate Agent and Bon Mot Communications, you step away from the safety, security, and guaranteed paycheck that comes with a senior executive position to become an entrepreneur.

Internally driven from an early age to excel at everything she did, Angelique was temporarily knocked off track by the diagnosis of Multiple Sclerosis (MS), a potentially debilitating genetic disease that attacks the central nervous system, at just 25 when she woke up to find she couldn't see. Taking stock of what she truly wanted to accomplish personally and professionally, she made the conscious decision to step off the corporate fast track and blaze her own trail. In relatively short order, she built a very successful corporate communications consultancy, working with a broad range of Fortune 500 companies in the defense, energy, high tech, e-commerce, medical and consumer products arenas, developing both internal and external strategic marketing and communications plans.

Complications arising from the birth of her twin boys, Brody and Chase, which left Angelique facing rapid heart failure, led to another re-evaluation of priorities and the eventual birth of her second company. While she enjoyed the communications work with her corporate clients, she felt deep down that something was missing and that she could have a much broader impact. She noticed that the vast majority of small business owners were trying to sell to other small business owners, leaving many smart, talented business owners struggling financially and exhausted physically and emotionally. She decided to leverage her own skill and experience landing lucrative corporate contracts and empower other women business owners to successfully tap into the lucrative $8 trillion plus corporate business-to-business market place.

After a bit of trial and error – including a failed business partnership – she developed The Corporate Agent to educate, train and support fellow small business owners on exactly how to package, market, and deliver their products and services to Fortune 1000 companies. The range of businesses she's helped break into corporate is nothing short of phenomenal – from health and wellness to specialty gifts to coaches to efficiency experts to performing artists and beyond. In addition, she's developed a remarkable values-based consultative selling approach that maintains authenticity and transparency during the sales process while delivering great results.

A firm believer in focusing on her brilliance while delegating, deferring, or deleting everything else, Angelique has built a formidable team consisting of both traditional employees and strategic outsourcing partners. Her favorite hires are fellow moms that are looking to create a lifestyle business that delivers excellent income while providing freedom and flexibility for family and friends.

Even though her business passed through the 7-figure mark, Angelique is not one to rest on her laurels. She's actively building a large number of collaborative partnerships with other small business owners, continually expanding her business and team, and looking for every opportunity to help other women entrepreneurs create extraordinary success without sacrificing who they are personally. She embodies many of the attributes we focus on throughout the book. Keep your eye on Angelique, because not only has she accomplished all this by just 36, but her next frontier is taking on the issue of peer bullying among young girls – an issue she faced personally and resulting emotions she used to fuel her to success.

You can find out more about Angelique by visiting www.thecorporateagent.com.

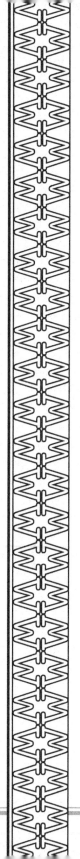

AUTHENTICITY RIPPLES

FABIENNE FREDRICKSON
Client Attraction System

Fabienne Fredrickson is an inspirational mentor to thousands of business owners worldwide, an author, international speaker and founder of The Client Attraction Business School™ and ClientAttraction.com, ranked repeatedly by *Inc.* magazine as one of America's Fastest Growing Private Companies. As one of the most influential marketing and success mindset thought-leaders and business coaches in the world, Fabienne's unique ability is getting entrepreneurs to take immediate marketing action on a systematic basis to produce dramatic results in less time than they would on their own. She's dedicated her life to helping entrepreneurs and business owners create a legacy of service through their business, adding value to the world in a lasting way and creating breakthrough paradigm shifts in their mindset and their personal income.

We love her voice and her story, so for this Meet the New Super Heroes, we wanted you to hear what she had to say in her own words. After you read it, you will understand why she has earned a spot on our list of the New Super Heroes.

I'm Fabienne Fredrickson, founder of The Client Attraction Business School™ and ClientAttraction.com, ranked repeatedly by Inc. *magazine as one of America's Fastest Growing Private Companies. I believe that entrepreneurs are catalysts for creating positive change in the world. Because of this, I believe it is the duty of the entrepreneur to play a bigger game in service to others and to create a lasting contribution. By educating, developing and inspiring my entrepreneurial clients to multiply their reach with authenticity, integrity and love, I help them realize their fullest potential and life purpose, while achieving their personal dreams and financial aspirations.*

I also believe that within every person is planted the seed and capability to be prosperous and abundant. It's called your message, your purpose, your life's work, your calling. When you say yes to your calling and get your message out in a big way, you attract the resources so you can keep doing it. This is not just the case for some people, it's true of all people—even you. You were born with a purpose: to move the planet forward and make the world a better place.

A defining moment in my life happened in late 1999. A few months before, I had quit my corporate job and had started a private nutrition practice out of my tiny apartment in New York City. I got clients right away, but not as many as I needed to pay the rent.

On one particular night, I woke up in a pool of sweat. All I kept saying to myself is, "What have I done? Why did I leave my well-paying corporate job just to struggle to get clients? How will I pay my rent if I don't get any more clients FAST?" I tossed and turned, and called my father in the middle of the night. He sat quietly listening to me. After I explained everything, he said, "Fabienne, if there's one thing I know about you, it's that when you want something, there's nothing that's going to stop you from getting it. So just figure out how you're going to get clients, and then go and do it."

At that very moment, I made a commitment to immerse myself in absolutely everything that had to do with getting clients. I read every book on marketing and networking I could get my hands on. I took every course that was available. I essentially decided to become a mini-expert on how to get clients.

Lo and behold, within less than 8 months, I had filled my private nutrition practice to full capacity: 31 clients.

During this process, I had an epiphany! The thing that I enjoyed MOST about my practice was actually the marketing, not teaching clients how to cook brown rice. But I also knew that deep within myself, there was a deep yearning to make a difference—to be a catalyst for others and the greater good.

Soon, my nutrition colleagues heard about my success and started taking me to the side and saying "Fabienne, how do you have 30 clients in less than a year and I have only 3? What am I doing wrong? Can you help me?" I'd give them two or three things to do and told them to call me in a few weeks to tell me how it went. Virtually every time, the nutritionist called me back a few weeks later saying "Hurray! I got a new client!!!!"

A year later, I closed down my nutrition practice, opened up ClientAttraction.com and made a commitment to dedicate the rest of my professional life to teaching other self-employed sole practitioners how get more clients in record time. Today, just a little over 10 years later, it has evolved into The Client Attraction Business School™, the largest of its kind in the world, and become a multi-million dollar business serving solo-entrepreneurs around the globe.

As a part of my work I host a 3-day Mindset Retreat™ every year in Florida, and in 2012, I invited my friend Cynthia Kersey to share the mission of her Unstoppable Foundation with my attendees. The Unstoppable Foundation is a non-profit humanitarian organization bringing sustainable education to children and communities in developing countries thereby creating a safer and more just world for everyone. Their mission is to ensure that every child has access to the lifelong gift of an education.

Within one hour of introducing Cynthia and her foundation at the event, the entire audience of our Mindset Retreat™ pitched in along with me and my husband Derek, and together we raised over $125,000 to build 5 schools in the Maasai Mara region of Kenya, Africa. Five schools, complete with education, water, how to grow crops, nutrition, alternative income and healthcare! This is the most Cynthia has ever raised at one event, and for that, I am eternally grateful for the extreme generosity of all those in my Mindset Retreat™ "tribe."

What's more, I then had the life-changing opportunity to take my daughter, Claire, and go with Cynthia to Kenya to witness first-hand the work on these five schools and to visit the children, their families, teachers and communities that these schools will serve.

People keep asking me how it was, how I was changed by my visit and how it is going to affect how I live my life and run my business… Up to now, I've had no words to fully describe how this experience has changed me. It's incredibly profound, an experience that's changed both Claire and me.

Apart from experiencing the children's joy in getting a real school and witnessing how much they believe that they (especially girls) have a RIGHT to learn, one of the major highlights for me was spending a week with the Maasai warriors who are famous for their fearless approach to life and unflinching courage.

My warrior friend Jackson spent hours with us over a period of 10 days sharing his culture and beliefs with me and taught me so much about courage and confronting fear (imagine regularly experiencing a lion staring you down within a few feet and what's required to survive and protect your cattle) and smiling through life, not allowing any worries to get you down, no matter what you have or don't have.

Claire and I would have gladly stayed for another 10 days, visiting more communities and getting to talk to the children attending the schools we're building in the Maasai Mara. They are so incredibly grateful to finally have a school to go to and are so committed to learning that several girls I talked with actually beg to go to school from 4am to 11pm each day, because they all want to go to University. Amazingly inspiring… That said, we really missed Derek and the boys, so coming home was total bliss! I'm planning on going again next year with my son Luc, to build more schools and meet more children. Contributing in this way has been a dream of mine for many years and watching it transform into reality overwhelms me with gratitude and fulfillment.

I believe that we all want to have a meaningful life. Creating a life of meaning and fulfillment is about living life like you mean it. A meaningful life is one where you leave a mark on society—when you put your head on the pillow at night and say, "Today was a good day. I made a difference in a life…." That's true fulfillment. Figure out what means most to you and focus on giving back in a way that fills your heart. You are not here to just exist but to create a ripple effect, in only the way you can.

You can learn more about Fabienne at www.ClientAttraction.com.

BLING YOUR WAY TO A BETTER WORLD

JESSICA HERRIN
CEO, Stella & Dot

Jessica Herrin is the founder of jewelry company Stella & Dot. Stella & Dot sold $100 million worth of jewelry in 2011, and is on track to sell over $1 billion by 2015. Her company is innovative, drawing from the old school model of Mary Kay and Tupperware, but taking that model into the 21st century by combining incredible, personalized service with an e-commerce platform and viral social media. Herrin calls it "social selling."

How does she do it? By empowering a veritable army of salespeople ("stylists") to sell the products for her in intimate, girlfriend driven trunk shows. Her stylists have become the brand evangelists for Stella & Dot, driving stunning yearly growth since she re-launched the company in 2007. Since that time, the company has paid out well over $100 million in commissions to its 20,000+ stylists.

This is the second successful startup for Herrin. She sold her first, WeddingChannel.com, to The Knot for $78 million in 2007. As WeddingChannel.com hit its stride, Oprah even had Jessica on her show and called her and her business partner women who "followed their hearts and found their fortunes."

Jessica was grateful for such success (she talks today about gratitude a lot these days, especially after doing work through the Stella & Dot foundation to build schools in Africa – as she says, "I have a floor! I can't complain about anything because I have a floor!") But grateful as she was for her success as an entrepreneur, she also felt conflicted about what it cost her. "For four years, I worked every night and weekend," she says. "I'd just married, and I never saw my husband. I wanted to start a family, but I couldn't see adding a baby to the picture."

When Herrin's husband was offered his dream job in Austin, Texas, she left WeddingChannel.com and became a senior manager in e-commerce at Dell computers. According to Jessica, "The job was challenging, but in a completely sane way." And after learning she was pregnant with her first child, she decided to turn to creating her dream business: "a company that you own but that doesn't own you."

Stella & Dot offers stylists a chance to be an entrepreneur. For $199 they get a starter kit with the supplies and samples they'll need to sell jewelry and handbags at trunk shows or on their own e-commerce websites. "Think of it as a 'business in a box,'" she says. It gives enormous opportunity to her stylists and many of them are multi-six figure success stories now. All of them tout the flexibility, fun and sisterhood that comes along with being a part of the Stella & Dot community.

When asked what advice she would give an aspiring entrepreneur, Jessica said, "The first and most relevant thing I can say is that being an entrepreneur must be your calling. It sounds lofty and grand but building a business takes so much commitment and effort. Only if you love it can you levitate yourself over the obstacles that stand in the way of creating a business. You need to be mission-driven and authentically connected to what you do. It's a heavy question, but if you are going to commit your time and your family's time and other people's money and your life to something, you should not just pursue it because it makes money. You should do it because it is uniquely suited for you. In retrospect, WeddingChannel.com was right for the time, and it was commercially exciting, but it wasn't my purpose. With Stella & Dot I feel like I'm in the happiness business. I bound out of bed every morning for the opportunity to do it all again."

Jessica has succeeded in making the business streets not only safe for herself and her family, but for the 20,000+ stylists who are a part of her brand. For that, she definitely has earned a spot on our New Super Hero list.

Reprinted from
http://www.gsb.stanford.edu/news/headlines/the-happiness-business.html

SHE'S COME A LONG WAY BABY

SUE HOPPIN
National Military Spouse Network

"You've come a long way, baby" is a perfect descriptor for author, entrepreneur, and social connector dynamo extraordinaire Sue Hoppin. Born in Laos, Sue emigrated to the U.S. with her family at the age of 6, after shortly after the Laotian government was overthrown in a communist coup in 1975. Even though English is a second language for Sue (her native languages are Laotian and French), she didn't let that slow her down and went on to excel academically at the prestigious Madeira Prep School in Virginia and the University of Denver, where she graduated with a degree in International Studies.

Shortly after graduation, she married Kevin Hoppin, a 1990 graduate of the United States Air Force Academy and embarked on a world-spanning adventure as a military spouse, with stops in Florida, Kansas, Okinawa and Germany before landing in DC. Along the way, she picked up a Master's Degree in International Relations, but found it challenging – as many military spouses do – to develop a sustainable professional career. However, Sue made strategic volunteering and community involvement a top priority wherever she went.

When her husband was re-assigned to Washington, Sue decided it was time to really start making an impact for military spouses and families and literally created her own position as the first Deputy Director of Military Spouse Outreach for the Military Officers Association of America (MOAA), one of the country's top military associations with membership of 375,000. She developed a wide array of innovative military spouse initiatives and was instrumental in forming MOAA's first Military Spouse Advisory Council. Concurrently, she co-authored the "A Family's Guide to the Military for Dummies" and was twice named to the "Who's Who of Military Spouses" list by Military Spouse magazine.

In 2010, she took the bold step of leaving her comfortable and secure position with MOAA and created the National Military Spouse Network (NMSN), an organization dedicated to fostering the professional development, portable careers, and entrepreneurial pursuits of fellow military spouses to support the all-volunteer military. A tireless advocate for military spouses and amazing connector of people and organizations, Sue excels at developing forward-thinking programs that meet the ever-changing needs of military spouses/families and is a sought-after consultant who advises corporations, non-profits, and government entities on how best to connect with – and serve – the military market.

Her annual NMSN Military Spouse Career Summit in Washington, DC is a dynamic, interactive professional development and educational event that connects military spouses with all the opportunities available to them and draws top-level speakers such as Craig Newmark, the Founder of Craigslist.com.

Most recently, Sue served on the Board of Directors for Blue Star Families from 2010–13 and was recently appointed by President Obama to the prestigious Board of Visitors for the United States Air Force Academy.

Find out more about Sue and the great work she does with military spouses at http://www.nationalmilitaryspousenetwork.org.

She is a shining example of Wonder Women who are making a difference through selfless service, innovation and vision.

LISA NICHOLS
Motivating the Masses

Lisa Nichols is CEO of Motivating the Masses, one of the top training and development companies in the world. She is a best-selling author of six books and one of the most sought-after transformational speakers whose global platform has reached and served millions.

But Lisa's path to success was far from smooth or easy, and it makes her accomplishments all that much more admirable and inspiring. As she says, "In order for me to tell you how good my life is, I have to tell you how much of a mess it was before. It's the only way you could adequately understand the miracle of my journey."

Lisa grew up in South Central LA in a large, poor African American family. Her parents were loving and attentive to her, and she says that they taught her to stand up for what she believed in, to be good to people, ad to appreciate and love family. She describes it as a wonderful way to grow up. But dark times lay ahead through her experience as one of the first African American students to be a part of the education integration process in Los Angeles. The program took inner-city kids and bussed them 40 miles to schools in traditionally white suburban neighborhoods. It was a great opportunity for a better education, but when she arrived on her first day, she was greeted by angry parents who yelled and threw eggs and tomatoes at her bus. From that day on, she was subject to constant ridicule and hatred from her classmates. In one compelling example, she describes a Charlie's Angels and Bionic Woman competition on her playground that she lost even though she was the best in the competition. When asked why she wasn't the winner, the other kids told her "Lisa, what hero have you ever seen who was black?"

The abuse and ridicule that she endured as a child (including being molested) led her to seriously contemplate and almost act on suicide. Thank goodness for all of us that she didn't follow through on those thoughts.

Her extraordinary story of transforming her own life from a struggling single mom on public assistance from South Central Los Angeles to now Millionaire Entrepreneur is the inspiration behind her bold mission to teach others that it is possible to do the same. Using her signature No Matter What! system (and based on her New York Times Bestseller by the same name), Lisa teaches people how to master accomplishing unfathomable goals and to tap their limitless potential.

According to Lisa, no matter what happens or what people say, you must commit to taking action and do what you need to do. And if you stumble along the way, you need "bounce-back muscles." More than anything, she wants women to be who they truly are, and to know that even though they aren't perfect, they have an important role to fill on this planet.

Today, Lisa is about to become the 7th woman to publicly list a company and has written 7 best sellers. She travels the world selling out auditoriums as she inspires people to rise up and reclaim their lives.

Her featured role in the movie *The Secret* catapulted her popularity across the globe. Lisa has since appeared on the "Oprah Winfrey Show," "Extra," "Larry King Live" and starred on NBC's Emmy Award-winning show, "Starting Over."

Coined "The Breakthrough Specialist" by her peers in the industry, her powerful message of empowerment, service, gratitude and excellence has been delivered via workshops and programs which have impacted the lives of millions of adults and over 200,000 teens through her non-profit foundation, Motivating the Teen Spirit.

Honored with numerous awards for her work, Lisa has received the Humanitarian Award from the country of South Africa, The Ambassador of Good Will Award, Emotional Literacy Award, and The Legoland Foundation's Heart of Learning Award. The City of Henderson, Nevada named November 20th as Motivating the Teen Spirit Day and the City of Houston, Texas named May 9th as Lisa Nichols Day for her dedication to service, philanthropy and healing.

As a founding member of the Transformational Leadership Council, Lisa joins other personal and organizational development luminaries such as Jack Canfield, Mark Victor Hansen, John DeMartini, Marci Shimoff and others to co-create value and learning that help people change their lives and change the planet.

As CEO of Motivating the Masses, Inc., Lisa Nichols leads a highly energetic, heart-centered and experienced team of business and leadership development master trainers and coaches who serve speakers, authors and entrepreneurs with world-class programs, masterminds and products. Lisa lives, plays and works in the greater San Diego, California area and on stages around the world.

Since *The Secret*, Lisa Nichols' powerful message of personal empowerment has helped thousands of people make significant, positive changes in their lives. Groups from corporate executives to teenagers have been motivated by Lisa Nichols' inspiring presentations, and she's been honored worldwide for her passion and drive. She is also the author of two of the best-selling Chicken Soup for the Soul books.

Her playground companions might have scoffed at Lisa filling the role of a hero, but they didn't know how wrong they were. Lisa Nichols is clearly a modern day Wonder Woman and a bona fide Super Hero.

To learn more about Lisa, visit
http://motivatingthemasses.com/

SEEK THE GREATER GOOD

JENNIFER LONGMORE
Soul Journeys

Jennifer Longmore, Forensic Investigator turned North America's Soul Purpose Expert, is the internationally acclaimed host of "Soul Purpose Central," 2-time best selling author, and creator of the Heal Your Money Story Intensive. For over 15 years and 20,000 soul purpose sessions, she has been helping people remember who they really are and to eliminate money as the #1 reason that they hold themselves back in life and business. Jennifer has empowered people through all walks of life, including a who's who of actors, professional athletes, CEOs of leading companies, and other influential luminaries.

Jennifer is a spiritual advisor (and a brilliant, gifted one at that), but what secures her a slot on our Wonder Women list is that she is also a savvy, laser focused, successful business woman. You might not think about a spiritual guru being someone who is also extremely wise about financial issues, but then you haven't met Jennifer. In fact, she is really what all Wonder Women should aspire to be: unceasingly generous and loving, while being unceasingly focused on building a financial and business legacy to boot (okay, she is Canadian...we had to say that).

Since launching her coaching practice 10 years ago, she has had incredible success on all levels – including a full practice within three months and building a six-figure business in just ten months from launching – but when you ask her what her ultimate mission is in life, she will tell you that she hopes to one day sell her business so she can devote her time to less fortunate children and animals. "I'm creating my business to sell so that I can have more time to give back and create various foundations that are close to my heart (ie. missing children, violence against women, microfinancing for women entrepreneurs in developing countries, saving endangered species)," says Jennifer.

Her success hasn't come easy, though. Says Jennifer: "When my practice was full after 3 months, I didn't know how to handle the volume. Not having the business savvy at the time, I turned folks away and referred them out rather than creating ways to serve more people such as hiring team members and creating group programs. BUT I now to get to teach others how to do that by saving themselves a lot of time and avoiding leaving so much money on the table."

The sincerity of her compassion and her deep commitment to doing right in the world can be seen in her early career as a forensic investigator, where she was assigned some of the most emotionally challenging cases involving violence to women and children. She was a superstar even then, rising through the ranks of her division as an unheard of young age. But the lifestyle, demands and emotional stress took its toll, and she found herself looking for a way to use her gifts that also took care of herself. She eventually found her way to spiritual, life and business coaching, and hasn't looked back.

Now, part of her mission is to make sure that all women entrepreneurs (and men) look their money in the eye. She wants to empower spiritual entrepreneurs to share their gifts with the world, and to do it in a way that doesn't create financial crisis or hardship. To her, healing your money story is the crucial step towards true success and having all that your heart desires.

Words of wisdom from Jennifer:

"Release the attachment to what others think of you, take imperfect action and create a routine to savor your accomplishments."

"Heal your money story so that you can reap what you've been working so hard for!"

Her favorite Super Powers: Integrity, Practical Spirituality, Being a Visionary

Says Jennifer: "Heal your relationship with money - the frequency, consistency and efficacy of your marketing efforts will directly reflect the health of this relationship."

To learn more about Jennifer, visit: www.souljourneys.ca

Do Well And Do Good:
B CORPORATIONS

If you want to amp your commitment to socially responsible business practices up a notch, then consider getting your business certified as an official B Corporation. http://www.bcorporation.net

B Corps are a new entity form that is committed to doing good beyond the bottom line. We love their mission statement, which is given in the form of the Declaration of Independence. It says:

WE ENVISION A NEW SECTOR OF THE ECONOMY which harnesses the power of private enterprise to create public benefit. This sector is comprised of a new type of corporation – the B Corporation – which is purpose-driven, and creates benefit for all stakeholders, not just shareholders.

As members of this emerging sector and as entrepreneurs and investors in B Corporations,

WE HOLD THESE TRUTHS TO BE SELF-EVIDENT:

That we must be the change we seek in the world.

That all business ought to be conducted as if people and place mattered.

That, through their products, practices, and profits, businesses should aspire to do no harm and benefit all.

To do so, requires that we act with the understanding that we are each dependent upon another and thus responsible for each other and future generations.

B Corps use the power of business to solve social and environmental problems. The B Corp website explains, "B Corp certification is to sustainable business what Fair Trade certification is to coffee or USDA Organic certification is to milk. B Corps are certified by the nonprofit B Lab to meet rigorous standards of social and environmental performance, accountability, and transparency. Today, there is a growing community of more than 760 Certified B Corps from 27 countries and 60 industries working together toward 1 unifying goal: to redefine success in business."

GREAT B-CORPORATION EXAMPLES:

Warby Parker is a NYC business founded in 2010 by Neil Blumenthal, Andrew Hunt, David Gilboa, and Jeffrey Raider. The foursome started the company when they were students at Wharton Business School and shortly after launching, they were featured on Vogue.com, and in GQ, which called it "the Netflix of eyewear." In the past few years, they have raised a bunch of money from investors including American Express and Mickey Drexler. Most notably, they are similar to Tom's Shoes in that for every pair of Warby Parker glasses purchased, a pair is given to someone in need. But unlike Tom's, Warby actually funds the production of a pair of eyeglasses by a non-profit organization which in turn sells either directly to consumers or companies. In July 2013, Warby Parker announced that it had distributed 500,000 pairs of eyeglasses to people in need. Warby Parker is a certified B Corp and is 100% carbon neutral.

Madcap Coffee Company in Grand Rapids, Michigan sells high quality specialty coffees, both wholesale and retail. The company is committed to socially responsible business practices. Instead of buying beans indirectly, Madcap works closely with farmers to improve crops, and can offer the farmers directly (instead of via middlemen) a better price since the farmers are providing a higher quality product. "Our role is to incentivize the farmers to pursue quality and experimentation through offering higher prices and commitments to buy their product," says Trevor Corlett, CEO and co-founder of Madcap. "Then in some cases [we] work side by side on the growing, harvesting and processing to continually try to achieve superior results." Both the farmers and Madcap benefit from this arrangement. In addition, Madcap pays above-average wages, and commits itself to zero waste through an aggressive composting and recycling program.

FAMOUS B CORPS
Ben & Jerry's, Plum Organics, Method, Patagonia, Etsy, Dansko, King Arthur Flour to name a few.

THE B CORP'S COUSIN
The L3C: The low-profit limited liability company – or L3C, is a relatively new legal entity that merges some of the attractive elements of the popular limited liability company (LLC), used by many start-up entrepreneurs and a 501(c)(3) non-profit. As of mid-2013, the LC3 was available in 9 states (Illinois, Louisiana, Maine, Michigan, North Carolina, Rhode Island, Utah, Vermont, and Wyoming) and several Indian nations. There are currently over 700 L3Cs in operation, with many more applications pending. In addition, L3C legislation has been introduced in 26 other states. As a result, this is another great options for entrepreneurs and business owners with a social mission to explore.

Think Global, Be Local

In the wake of the Great Recession and the questionable business choices of the leaders of many of the larger corporations in the US (ranging the gamut from unethical lending practices, to overt discriminatory policies and low pay, to polluting our food supply and more), there is a growing movement to shop local. Even American Express is getting in on it with its Small Business Saturday® event, now in its third year. Business owners like you can take on this same mission by working to build and foster your local communities.

One example of a business doing this well is **SAVOR SPA** in New York City, owned by Angela Jia Kim (one of our New Super Heroes). Angela has an in-spa boutique that sells only products created by local businesswomen in New York State. It is an incredible way to help promote local businesses and local women business owners, and the products offered are beautiful and yummy. **www.savorspa.com**

Another example of putting the local community first is the community organizations that are cropping up around the country, such as **LOCAL FIRST** in Grand Rapids Michigan. Local First is one of "a new kind of trade organization, which represents Main Street businesses that are committed to nurturing vibrant local economies as part of their business strategy." We've included their mission and values statements here so you can see an example of a group of people working for outcomes beyond the bottom line. They are definitely bringing their humanity and integrity to the office every day. **www.localfirst.com**

LOCAL FIRST MISSION STATEMENT:
We foster the development of an economy, grounded in local ownership, which functions in harmony with our ecosystem, meets the basic needs of our people, encourages joyful community life, and builds wealth.

VISION:

A community built around unique experiences that support a high quality life.

An economy that meets the needs of the people of our region and improves the environmental sustainability of our place.

A culture of collaboration that allows diverse parts of our community entrepreneurial success by capitalizing, supporting, and growing locally-owned businesses.

A future in which businesses, consumers, and employees recognize their interconnectedness and see themselves as investors in the quality of life for West Michigan residents.

Being an international leader in sustainable economic and community development

VALUES:

Local independent ownership
Human scale relationships
Entrepreneurship
Creativity
Social and monetary capital
Natural environment and resources
Joyful experiences

THEREFORE, WE [ARE]

Actively encouraging the creation of a sustainable local economy through community education, relationship building, and normalizing behaviors.

Building, developing, and sustaining an environment in which local businesses grow and thrive.

Educating consumers and business owners about the benefits of spending their money at locally-owned businesses.

Educating local businesses about the ways in which positive employment practices, involvement in the community, and protecting the environment help them reach their goals and make them more effective community stewards.

We hope these stories have inspired you to action. Clearly, there are many courageous and visionary business owners out there daring to change the world one business at a time. They are striving to bring their humanity to the workplace and not just do well, but do good.

This is the future of our economy. And YOU are key to its success.

Spend some time thinking through how you can build integrity or doing good into your business. Create a mission statement that encapsulates that. And then map out the steps you can start taking today to transform not only our own life (like Arianna Huffington did), but the lives of your team members, clients or customers, and fellow community members. We promise that if you follow the advice we are giving you in this book, you will also do well financially. **You will not have to choose between doing well and doing good.**

"As we look ahead into the next century, leaders will be those who empower others."

– Bill Gates

ACTION ITEM CHECKLIST

Set aside 1-2 hours for these exercises and make sure you carve out some focused, uninterrupted time for this. These decisions are integral to creating the kind of business and kind of lifestyle that will be fulfilling for you. Don't be tempted to skip ahead and do this later. Everything we talk about later in the book is premised on the assumption that you have done this work. This is foundational work for the kind of business that will help save the economy and the world. Get your journal, iPad or laptop out and make these exercises really count!

☐ **EXERCISE ONE:** Write down three to five passions, interests, or desires that you regularly "check at the door" at work (either previously in your career or currently, whichever applies). Spend 15 minutes thinking about how you can stop leaving them at the door and begin working them into what you and your team members can do to incorporate these back into your daily work.

☐ **EXERCISE TWO:** In Super Power One, we encouraged you to write your own personal mission statement. Now it is time to use that to write your company's new mission statement. We gave you some great examples in the last Super Power section of company mission statements, and some great stories in this section about the why behind many successful, socially conscious businesses. So use all of those as inspiration for your own company's mission.

☐ **BONUS**: If you are so inclined, sit down and think about the greater good you would like for your company to accomplish. Then, list three charities or social causes that you love and jot down 5 ways you can support each of their efforts through your personal and/or professional endeavors.

Examples:

• *Do you want to donate a portion of your revenue to a charity?*

• *Would you like to start your own foundation and not just donate, but raise money to support these causes?*

• *Would you prefer to keep business and charitable work separate and pursue these things in your off hours with your own personal money?*

NOTES

4

cu·ri·os·i·ty, n.

ʊ**W**

1. An eager desire to know or learn; inquisitiveness;

2. Marked by desire to investigate and learn;

3. *The Wonder Women Way:* You have to want to know the truth to have a real and sustainable business. Being curious and not afraid of the numbers is powerful; it encapsulates initiative, wisdom, courage, transparency, determination.

CURIOSITY

Know Your Numbers

Have you ever watched Shark Tank? How many of those people who are pitching for investment money don't know how to answer questions from the Sharks about their business finances? They stand there looking uncomfortable, eyes to the ceiling as they attempt to crunch some numbers in their head right on the spot.

The truth is that if you are really a business owner, you could answer those types of questions on the fly.

A fool and his money are easily parted.

– Irish Proverb

You as the founder of your company must know your costs, your margins, your profit and loss. You must be intimately knowledgeable of what is coming in and going out on a daily basis. You need to develop realistic expectations of when and how money will come in. Do you get paid by the hour, the project, or milestones? How will you allocate this money to the running of your business? What will go to bills, what will go to employees, and what will be left over to support your family? What will it require of you personally to keep it going?

DON'T BE AFRAID TO TALK MONEY

Money can be a touchy subject, especially among women. Entrepreneurs can often get so wrapped up in the potential of their dream that they completely overlook making strategic financial decisions.

However, finances are not just something you can figure out as you go along—you must look at the numbers frequently and in detail. You must see where money is going out, and where it is coming in.

DEMYSTIFYING $$

So you are ready to look your money in the eye. So how do you do that? Even starting can be intimidating if you don't have any experience with it. So we are going to do a super condensed tutorial here to get you started. There is a lot more to say on these topics, and we encourage you to become a student of your business' finances, but this chapter will get you launched in the right direction. Take a deep breath and read on!

ARE YOU MAKING ANY MONEY?

First and foremost, you must determine how much you will charge for your offerings. That decision is slightly different for service-based businesses than it is for product-based businesses, but one thing is constant between the two: **You must price your offerings in a way that covers your costs, overhead and enough profit margin that you are actually healthy financially.** If you underprice your services or goods, you will never get ahead and your company will be perpetually sick and anemic, or it might flat-line.

YOUR SERVICES

If you are offering a service, like accounting, coaching or anything else that is based on your time and effort, then there are likely two ways you are pricing things: hourly or project-based. For those of us in the service-industry, either pricing model is likely based on an assumed hourly rate and an estimated number of hours that it will take to deliver the service. One of the biggest mistakes we see when people price their services is choosing an hourly or project-based price that is based on what others are charging in their industry or what they *think* their clients will pay, instead of basing if on the value of their service to their clients.

While it is important to not price yourself out of the market with your rates, basing what you charge on what a competitor charges is like throwing a dart at a dartboard. **You need to do more than guess that your prices should be or what you think a client will pay you for your prices.**

PRICING: *Service-Based Businesses!*

What to include in your pricing model:

1. The direct costs of delivering your service. If you have a staff member doing some or all of the work for the client, what do you have to pay them to do the work? These are your labor costs. Note: What you pay a staff member should be lower than what you charge the client, because – as we are saying here – you must build in a profit to your pricing!

2. Any indirect costs, like rent, utilities, Internet, administrative costs, administrative staff salaries and benefits, taxes, insurance, depreciation, advertising, office supplies, and other overhead costs. If you fail to include the cost of doing business, you will never make enough money to break even. That is a clear recipe for bankruptcy.

3. Your costs should also include YOUR salary. If you don't price your services to include a reasonable salary for yourself, you will never be able to get paid for what you do, no matter how many clients you have.

4. Profit. Yes, you are in the business to make a profit. To be clear, a profit is what you take in AFTER all of your costs are paid. So if you don't charge enough to cover your costs, you will never have a profit.

5. Finally, you need to take into account the VALUE of what you offer, not just costs. It might not cost you as much to deliver a service that has exponential value to your client. There is no rule that your pricing should give you a small profit margin. If what you do is extremely valuable to your client, price based on the *value*.

A SHIRT BY ANY OTHER NAME

There could be a wide range of pricing options in your industry, depending on the quality of your goods and what your target market is. For example, Target sells shirts and so does Ralph Lauren. It is likely that they have very similar costs to produce their shirts (although Ralph Lauren is probably using better materials, which would increase his costs a bit). But Target's demographic expects affordable pricing, and Ralph Lauren's expects to pay a lot for the privilege of wearing a designer label. So obviously, their retail prices are very different. As a result, Ralph's profit margins are going to be much higher than Target's per shirt.

And once you have your costs and pricing and margins figured out (piece of cake, right?), then you can begin to drill down to a deeper level of understanding as you operate and that understanding will ensure even greater financial health for you and your business....

PRICING: *Products and Goods!*

Pricing your goods is a bit more complicated than pricing a service. It's important to make sure you are set up to make a good profit (and a living!) because you have additional costs that don't apply to service-based companies. Here is what to include:

1. Prototype development. In a product-based business, you will be incurring costs to develop the good your want to sell. That process of developing a market-ready prototype costs money. Generally, these costs are factored (or divided) over a certain number of goods (usually an estimate of how many you will sell that season).

2. Material costs. You must track very precisely what it costs you to purchase the materials that go into making your product. If those amounts are not factored in, you will never have a sustainable profit margin and you won't survive as you grow. If you don't make a profit on one widget, you won't make one on a million. Get a profit built into your prices now so that as you scale, you will know you have a predictable profit margin.

3. Labor costs. If you have a staff member or vendor doing some or all of the work to make or manufacture your goods, what do you have to pay them to do the work? These are your labor costs. Obviously, these are direct costs to produce your good and must be included in your pricing if you want to survive.

4. If you are a retailer instead of a creator of goods, then your pricing is slightly different. In that case, you will be paying a wholesale price for the goods you want to sell instead of product development, material and labor costs for production. So your cost will be that wholesale price. Your margins will need to set a high enough retail price in your store to cover your costs, including that wholesale price for your goods.

5. **For both creators of goods and retailers, you need to factor in any indirect costs,** like rent, utilities, Internet, administrative costs, administrative staff salaries and benefits, taxes, insurance, depreciation, advertising, office supplies, and other overhead costs. If you fail to include the cost of doing business, you will never make enough money to break even. That is a clear recipe for bankruptcy.

6. **Just as with a services-based business, your costs should also include YOUR salary.** If you don't price your services to include a reasonable salary for yourself, you will never be able to get paid for what you do.

7. **Profit. Yes, you are in the business to make a profit.** To be clear, a profit is what you take in AFTER all of your costs are paid. So if you don't charge enough to cover your costs, you will never have a profit. Each industry has a typical profit margin for wholesale and one for retail. Get to know your industry, so you know what ballpark you need to be in so that you don't price yourself out of the market. Make sure that if your industry has a specific price point (meaning, you will not be able to sell your goods wholesale to a retailer for more than a specific amount), then you will have to find a way to cut your costs in order to make sure you still make your margins.

For more guidance on this, come visit us at
www.wonderwomenbook.com/moneytalk

Now don't let your eyes glaze over...

We promise you that you'll start to fall in love with your business numbers – or at least be willing to go on a blind date with them – after we share the power of what a few simple numbers can show you. Why is this so important? Here are three fundamental – and sobering – business truths you'll be stuck with if you don't learn to love your basic business numbers:

TRUTH #1: Your business will struggle mightily to ever get past the micro-business stage. Any real level of business growth is virtually impossible if you don't have a firm grasp of your basic business numbers.

TRUTH #2: Your business will be plagued with hidden "money leaks" that will drain thousands, hundreds of thousands or even millions of dollars of net personal business income from your pocket over the life of your business.

TRUTH #3: If you ever want to sell business in the future, you must have a good grasp of the financials (and good financial systems) to make the business attractive to an outside buyer (and not get taken to the cleaners on the sale).

KBMs vary from business to business, depending on: size, whether you're a service-based business or product-based business, whether you're selling to consumers or other businesses, etc. The fundamental KBMs every business owner and entrepreneur should understand are the Profit & Loss (P&L) and Cash Flow statements:

PROFIT & LOSS (P&L) STATEMENT

Also known as an "income statement" or "income & loss statement," the simplest definition of an P&L is that it summarizes the revenues, cost, and expenses incurred in running your business over a specific period (weekly, monthly, quarterly, or annually). It reflects the ability of your company to actually generate profit and you can use the P&L to model the impact of increasing revenue and/or reducing expenses. We've encountered many business owners that have really good revenue coming into their business, but after all that initial income filters through the business…there's very little left for the business owner to put in her pocket. Why? Too many "money leaks!" A quick read of a good P&L can rapidly ID money leaks and areas that you can improve the profitability of your business.

CASH FLOW STATEMENT

A kissing cousin of the P&L, the Cash Flow statement tracks the actual inflow of revenues, outflow of expenses over a given period (daily, weekly, monthly, quarterly, or annually), along with the current amount of available cash in your business at any given time. While a cash flow statement won't tell you whether or not your business will be profitable over the long-term, it's invaluable in the daily management of the business. This is particularly true if your business income acts like ocean tides, with periods of high income interspersed with periods of low income. Making a big expenditure when your business income is at low tide can leave you unable to cover other business expenses, which can lead to bounced checks and angry bankers!

Unfortunately, most small business owners and entrepreneurs stop at the P&L and Cash Flow statements when looking at their KBMs and never unlock the hidden power of other KBMs that are critical to the long-term success of your business. Let's take a look at a few important KBMs by category:

SALES

- Gross sales/revenue/income per team member
- Prospect to customer/client conversion ratio
- Average revenue per customer/client
- Average number of sales per customer/client
- Average net profit per unit sale

MARKETING

- Average customer/client acquisition cost
- Average qualified lead acquisition cost
- Customer/client satisfaction rate
- Customer/client retention rate
- Customer/client click-thru or open rates

OPERATIONS

- Team member satisfaction or engagement level
- Expense per team member
- Billable hours to total hours ratio
- Team member turnover ratio
- Order fill rate

FINANCIAL

- Net profit per team member
- Accounts receivable (A/R) average days to payment
- A/R over 45 days
- Average monthly overhead
- Inventory turnover by unit

These are just of few of the more than 100 different KBMs we identified while researching this book. At this point, you may be asking yourself "Nice list...but what does it actually mean?"

Glad you asked!

PROFIT MARGIN: The amount by which revenue from sales exceeds costs in a business.

GROSS REVENUE: The amount of money that is brought into a company by its business activities. Also called Gross Profit.

NET REVENUE: Gross Revenue minus all operating costs, such as wages, overhead, and depreciation. Also called Net Profit.

OVERHEAD: The operating expenses of a business, such as rent, utilities and taxes, but not including labor and materials (which are direct costs).

COST OF GOODS SOLD (COGS): The direct costs of production of the goods sold by a company, including materials and labor used to produce the good. It does not include indirect costs such as distribution or sales force costs. COGS are deducted from Gross Revenue to determine a company's gross margin.

GROSS MARGIN: A company's total sales revenue minus its cost of goods sold, divided by the total sales revenue, expressed as a percentage. The gross margin represents the percent of total sales revenue that the company retains after incurring the direct costs associated with producing the goods and services sold by a company. The higher the percentage, the more the company retains on each dollar of sales to service its other costs and obligations.

$$\text{Gross Margin (\%)} = \frac{\text{Revenue} - \text{Cost of Goods Sold}}{\text{Revenue}}$$

KBM: Simply, measurements of business activity. Business Metrics that provide you with key information about your performance.

T12M: The Trailing 12 Months (T12M) chart, developed by Kraig Kramers – founder of CEO Tools – can help you track monthly sales for your last 12 months. T12M charts graphically tell you whether you're improving or slipping.

As Robin S. Sharma states so eloquently in *The Greatness Guide: Powerful Secrets for Getting to World Class* (Harper Collins, 2006), "What gets measured gets improved."

If you're not tracking any of your KBMs, it's really hard to figure out problem areas and where you can make immediate improvements with very little effort.

Let's take a quick look at an example:

THE CASH FLOW CRUNCH

Mary is a corporate refugee who jumped ship 2 years ago to start her own consulting firm to focus on her core strengths and create greater schedule flexibility for her family. She's landed some good clients and by the amount she's invoicing, she should be doing well on paper, but she feels really stretched some months just to meet her basic business overhead and is getting stressed and frustrated.

Mary started tracking several KBMs, including:
- Monthly cash flow for the previous 12 months
- Billable hours to total hours ratio
- Accounts billable average days to payment

She quickly uncovered a couple of important issues:

CHALLENGE #1: Her Accounts Receivable (A/R) average days to payment was a whopping 70 days from invoice to payment and she spent a number of hours chasing after clients to get payments.

CHALLENGE #2: Her billable hours to total hours ratio was shockingly low…under 20%. She'd gotten involved in a number of business networking groups and charity boards that were sucking up a lot of time for which she wasn't getting paid.

CHALLENGE #3: She discovered her cash flow showed some very clear ebbs/flows – with spring/fall being her big revenue peaks and summer/winter being her revenue valleys. Several of her biggest expenses, including several big professional software license renewals, coincided with her lowest revenue periods.

Armed with this knowledge, Mary was able to make several small changes that greatly improved her business – along with greatly lowering her stress level – including:

SOLUTION #1: To reduce her A/R issue, Mary instituted an 18% annual finance charge (1.5% per month) on all A/R over 30 days. In addition, she increased her engagement agreement deposit from 33% to 50%. Finally, she talked to several of her clients and found they greatly preferred to pay by credit card (which she had been avoiding due to the fees) and that most credit card invoices were paid immediately on receipt. She realized that the fees for accepting credit cards were smaller that the time and money she lost in chasing clients for payment, so she signed up for a credit card merchant account immediately!

SOLUTION #2: Mary committed to increasing her billable hours to total hours ratio to at least 40% over the next 6 months and strategically assessed all of her external involvements for their business generating and visibility potential. As a result, she reduced her external monthly commitments from 7 to 3 hours and refocused the 12 hours per month she freed up on direct marketing to prospects and centers of influence.

SOLUTION #3: She contacted the vendors for her large ticket renewal items and moved the renewal dates to coincide with her peak positive cash flow periods. In addition, she set-up a small business line-of-credit to handle any unforeseen situations.

Without measuring some simple KBMs and then using that information to take proactive action, Mary would still be stuck and frustrated. The positive benefits of tracking even a few KBMs in your business are enormous and we suggest you start doing so immediately!

At the simplest level, KBMs are a snapshot that shows where your business is with regards to that metric at a particular point in time. However, the true power of KBMs is revealed when you start using the 12-month Moving Average or Trailing 12-Months (T12M, for short).

T12Ms are created by taking the of the current month of any KBM, adding the previous 11 months of that KBM and then dividing that total by 12. For instance, if the total revenues for your business for the current month plus the preceding 11 months are $1.5 million, then your T12M is $125,000 ($1.5 million/12). T12Ms can easily be created for virtually any KBM using a simple spreadsheet. **Why is the T12M so important?** While your regular KBMs are snapshots in time, the T12M shows trends and can help you spot opportunities or challenges in your business before they actually occur.

For example, award-winning serial entrepreneur Larry Broughton, founder and CEO of broughtonHOTELS and several other companies, credits the strategic use of T12Ms with helping his boutique hotel company sidestep the worst of the 2007–2009 financial downturn, "We noticed some alarming trends in several of our most important T12M metrics in early 2007 and could actually see the downturn coming.

We used that information to put together a 'recession proof' business plan and take action before bottom fell out. A lot of our hotel investors thought we were crazy when we put this plan in action in mid-2007... but we looked like geniuses when the downturn hit and were able to take advantage of a number of great acquisition opportunities while everyone else was paralyzed by fear and doubt."

In other words, tracking your T12Ms can save your business.

The two charts on the following page come from the same company and are a real world example.

ORDINARY MONTHLY CHART is the regular monthly sales chart, which reflects a big dip during the middle of the last recession. However, it looks like the overall sales are improving somewhat during mid-2008 and again in mid-2009 (after a typical seasonal dip around the holidays.

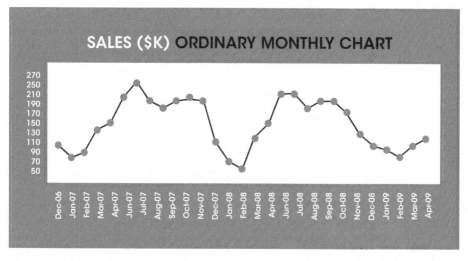

T12 CHART, which represents the same company's T12M, shows a completely different story. The trend line for sales is actually very bad...and heading back down in mid-2009. The T12M shows sales heading off the cliff, indicating it's time to take serious action. **Remember, folks, the numbers don't lie!**

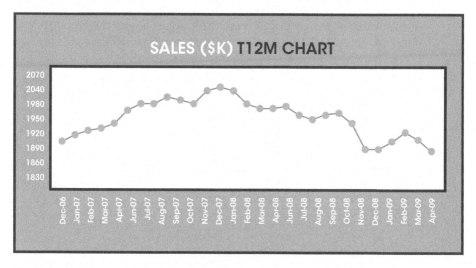

If you're not tracking your most important KBMs and not using the T12M measurement for those metrics, you're missing out on critical, actionable information that can literally save your business from impending doom or alert you to a golden opportunity. Try 'em...you'll like 'em!

The Incredible Power of Small Changes

If your business is facing revenue or sales challenges – like the company in the charts above – there are really only three ways to increase sales:

WAY #1: Get more customers/clients through effective marketing

WAY #2: Increase your revenue from existing clients by raising your rates, upselling them a more expensive version of the product/service they are currently using, or using add-ons to sell them additional products/services

WAY #3: Increase the frequency at which customers/clients buy from you

That's basically it... it doesn't get much simpler than that!

Unfortunately, most businesses focus on the first option – get more customers/clients – while ignoring the others. For most business, getting new customers/clients is much more expensive and time consuming than either selling more to current customers/clients or increasing the frequency with which you sell to them. Business is hard enough without making it harder, so make sure you pay attention to your current customers/clients (we're talking to you, cable TV companies)! Provide the best customer service or client care you can. Ask them about how you are doing or how you can improve their experience, *and then deliver!* The smartest thing you will ever do is keep current customers or clients happy. Not only will they bring you repeat business, but they will also become a source of referral work.

FORTUNATELY, IT ONLY TAKES SMALL CHANGES TO YIELD BIG JUMPS IN REVENUE. For instance, let's say your company has 1,000 clients that buy your $100 product/service and average of two times per year. In this case, your gross revenues would be $200,000 (1,000 clients x $100/unit x 2 times per year = $200,000). If you were able to increase each of these parameters by 10 percent – increasing your clients to 1,100, the price of your products/service to $110 and increased the annual frequency to 2.2 times per year, your gross revenue would jump by 33 percent to $266,000 annually (1,100 x $110 x 2.2 times per year = $266,000), as shown on the first line of the table below.

| | 1,000 | $100 | X2 | $200K | |
IMPROVE	# OF CLIENTS	$ PER TRANSACTION	# OF TRANSACTIONS	TOTAL	INCREASE
10%	1,100	$110	X2.2	$266K	33.1%
33%	1,330	$133	X2.66	$460	230%
50%	1,500	$150	X3	$675	337.5%
X2	2,000	$200	X4	$1.6M	800%
X3	3,000	$300	X6	$5.4 M	2,700%

Used with Permission. Copyright ©2012 Larry Broughton. All rights Reserved.

Just take a look at the enormous cumulative impact on revenues of relatively small changes. Take a moment and calculate how much just a 33% cumulative increase in revenue would mean to your business (and life). Just as in saving and investing, the compound effect of small positive changes, repeatedly frequently, can be huge!

There are two additional areas that you need to look at to determine where the leaks might be coming from: Legal and Hiring Expenses.

LEGAL

It might surprise you to learn that a huge source of money leaks can come from your legal foundation (or lack of one). Now, you might not have thought of your legal foundation as having anything to do with the money in your business, but it actually has EVERYTHING to do with it. **That is because when you don't have a proper legal foundation in place, you have a compromised foundation under your business.** Have you ever heard of what happens when a house has a foundation problem? It is something that must get fixed ASAP and that is extremely expensive to fix. But if you don't fix it, you could lose your entire house. Well, the same is true for the legal foundation of your business.

EXAMPLE: Say you launch a business and spend hours coming up with just the right name for your brand. You ask friends, colleagues and clients and are sure you have found the perfect name to express what you do. You buy the URL and pay a great graphic designer to create the perfect logo and website for your business. You start operating and have great success. People are responding to your brand and you are on your way. However, you decide not to spend the money on hiring a lawyer to search to make sure the name is actually available to you and you skip hiring that same lawyer to help you get a federal trademark because at $1500 (for example) it is all pretty expensive and you just don't have the cash flow right now to justify it. You are tired of hemorrhaging money, and after paying your graphic designer several thousand for your logo and website, you are done spending money. So you skip the trademark.

Two years later, you get a Cease and Desist letter in the mail telling you that you are actually infringing on a competitor's brand and that you have to stop using the name of your brand immediately. Now you have no choice but to hire a lawyer...to the tune of $10,000, $20,000 or $30,000 (or more if you end up in litigation and try to win the rights to your name). And if you lose, you have to rebrand. That means you not only incur the legal fees, but the cost of a new logo and website.

But most importantly, you have to start at square one with branding and recreating good will and brand reputation with your clients and the public. They will have to be re-educated about who your company is and what you do: All because you decided to skip the $1500 investment in preserving your rights to use that brand name. Do you see how having just one part of your legal foundation missing can be a HUGE money leak waiting to happen?

So, what do you need to address with your legal foundation? By now you have a good idea, since we have you a very detailed roadmap under Super Power Two! So go back and re-read that chapter, and take it seriously this time. Your future self will thank you for having the foresight to prevent expensive issues now.

HIRING AND DELEGATING

The second potential area of a money leak in your business has to do with your business expenses – much of this we have already covered under our discussion of KBMs. But one thing we didn't get into detail about and one of the biggest areas we see routinely causing business owners issues, especially in the service-based businesses we work with, is the issue of hiring and delegating.

Hiring and Delegating Too Soon: We all hear over and over that the best way to build your business is to focus on your zone of genius and delegate the rest to people who are experts in that type of work. And this is actually very good advice…but it only applies after you have had some initial success in your business. We hear a lot of "business gurus" out there telling you this, but we are here to tell you the truth.

The truth is that when you first start a business, you have no choice but to wear all hats. It is just the nature of getting a company off the ground. And we think it is a really good thing, because by doing everything in your business, you learn it intimately from the ground up. And by learning about your business from the ground up, you can make the kind of tweaks and course corrections that will improve your business and your brand, and will improve your clients or customers' experience. So don't rush to hire and delegate too soon or your will actually jip yourself out of a critical experienced as a business owner.

When to Hire or Delegate: When is the best time to hire or delegate? We are a bit old school about this because that is only because we've learned our lessons about this the hard way. And we would love to save you the trouble, so here is what we know: The best way to build a business is to focus on the number one most important thing and that is getting clients and/or customers. Of course, you have to have something to sell or offer them, so there is certainly work that goes into your infrastructure and systems (for more on that, visit us at www.wonderwomenbook.com/operationalwisdom), but once you have a solid foundation and infrastructure to support your offerings, then your focus has to be simply on getting clients or customers.

How do you do that? You start with one at a time and you make sure that once you have won that first client over, you provide them with such an incredible experience that it is a no brainer for them to return again and again and to refer you to another client or customer. And when that referred client or customer buys from you, you give them an exceptional experience. And so on. The result is that very quickly you will be getting a lot of work just by virtue of being incredible at what you do because you will be getting repeat business and referrals. Those are two of the main ways you build a company (the other is by increasing the number of items or the dollar amount each client or customer buys).

EXAMPLE: Kathleen, passionate about her product, hired on several team members at once to help her carry the load. However, she hired too many—while she could afford to pay them every month, there was nothing left over for herself. Upon examining her client list with a business coach, she found that two-thirds of her clients were actually costing her money each and every month—in a roundabout way, she was paying to work for them! Her business model simply could not survive. With the help of her coach, she pinpointed her favorite clients and their commonalities, those she made the most money from, and she examined which of her team she needed to support those particular clients. She also developed a structure to address all clients, not a different approach for each one. After readjusting the size of her team, her net income went from 5% to over 40% in a very short period of time. Kathleen's story is a perfect example of the pitfalls of ignoring the financial side and focusing solely on clients.

Is It Time to Hire or Delegate? Well, the way to know takes two separate assessments (and it goes back to looking your money in the eye). First, you need to be sure that when you price your service or product, you have factored in your costs, as we discussed above. There are many business coaches who will tell you to keep raising your rates, and there are certainly times to do this (like when you have a waiting list for clients and you have such a reputation that it makes sense you're your rates would reflect how in demand you are – that is simple economics). But for most types of companies, the price point you enter the market in is where you will have to stay. For example, if you are Banana Republic and you start selling shirts for $75 a piece, and that is how you become known among your customers, how do you think your customers would respond if you all of a sudden increased the price of your shirts to $200? Would that go over well? No. So when setting your prices, be realistic about how much your costs are so you factor those in from day one (some of that will require projecting costs since you have to anticipate what your costs will be).

And, as we discussed earlier in this chapter, make sure you also factor in some profit over an above your costs so that you can actually grow. If you price things so that they only cover your costs, you will stagnate and never grow. So, assuming your pricing has costs and profit factored in, then when you get to the point where you have so much client work or so many sales that you are unable to handle all of the work yourself, that is when you start to hire. But if the cost of that staff member isn't factored into your pricing, then paying them will eat into your profits. So make sure you really look your money in the eye early on so that hiring improves your business and doesn't make it anemic.

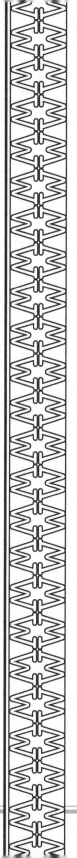

THE EVENT ELEPHANT IN THE ROOM:

Here is a question for you: Are you someone who travels many times a year to go to conferences and events for entrepreneurs or coaches? Is that really a good use of your money? Now, we don't have a problem with coaches (we've had and have excellent ones and believe in them wholeheartedly) and we don't have a problem with live events. But what we have seen is a tendency (especially among women entrepreneurs) to almost have an addiction to attending events. But then when the business owner gets there, she doesn't use the time to develop new clients or develop a strong relationship with a center of influence who would introduce them to a new universe of potential clients. As a result, the event just sucks money out of your business without refilling the empty tank.

Here is the rule of thumb with live events. Since they usually cost between $2000–4000 to attend (with airfare, hotel, food and the cost of the event), you'd better be darn sure that attending the event is going to result in making at least the cost of the trip in new business from the event.

This means your approach to the event needs to be very strategic and you need to set a goal for how many clients you need to attract and convert before the weekend is over. If you aren't able or willing to do that, you have no business attending that event (unless you are okay with allowing money to continue leaking out of your business...and a serious business owner would never be okay with that).

So, that is it! Are you still with us? Look, let's make it really simple in conclusion. Just look at how your expenditures in your biz are leading to increased revenue and profits. Anything that isn't contributing to that needs to be cut. And this is something you have to look at all the time. Not just once. Not just yearly. Not just monthly. Track it all the time. Look your money in the eye. You should know your expenses cold and should be reviewing a report of them weekly for your biz. If you aren't, start. That is the only way to know how to plug the actual money leaks in your business and grow, grow, grow!

☐ If you don't have a bookkeeper or accountant, get one! Business is tough enough without hamstringing yourself right out of the gate by not tracking your income and expenses.

☐ Determine EXACTLY how much it costs to deliver your product/service and then use that information to correctly price your product/service. Don't forget things like development costs, research, travel time, answering follow-up questions. Far too many new business owners set their prices too low and end up needlessly losing money. Pricing models are critical!

☐ Refer to the list of KBMs in this section and determine 2–3 that you should be tracking in your business...and start tracking them!

☐ Revist the 3-column Exercise and choose the top 2 items you need to delegate immediately and determine who you're going to hire or outsource this to.

NOTES

cre·a·tiv·i·ty, n.

1. The quality of having the ability or power to create;

2. The ability to be productive; creating rather than imitating;

3. Characterized by originality and expressiveness; imaginative;

4. Productive originality;

5. *The Wonder Women Way:* Creativity is at the core of having a strong team - creating an environment that enables and fosters creativity, in yourself and in your team.

CREATIVITY

Just Say No to Mini-Mes and Worker Bees

Like it or not, we are in the information and innovation age. In order to survive and thrive in the new economy, we have to be creative.

In fact, creativity is central to our success. We need to be creative leaders and creative bosses. Creativity is one of your most important Super Powers as a new Wonder Woman. That is because we need to figure out a way to enable our teams to be creative innovators and problem solvers. If our team members feel the freedom to be creative, it will be transformational for your business. A creative team is THAT important.

Focus on ideas, product, execution and your team. If you do this, the money will ultimately come. People who focus on finance generally fail.

– Richard Branson, Founder of Virgin Group

If we can impart you with one bit of wisdom for building your team it is this: When choosing a team, don't choose a mini-me or a worker bee. You want a creative thinker who balances out your strengths.

 Throughout this book, we use the term "team member" instead of "employee." Why? We believe that team member is much more appropriately and accurately describes the proper relationship in the collaborative economy we're in. The word employee is - in our humble opinion - obsolete and describes a subservient relationship that is all about power and control. Remember, we don't want serfs or drones, we want empowered, autonomous team members that can achieve the extraordinary!

NO MINI-MES

The heart of collaborative capitalism is about focusing on your own strengths and creating opportunities for those strengths to shine, while also creating opportunities for others to do the exact same thing. The key to this is building a collaborative team, with the perfect blend of talents that results in an optimum whole.

In other words, find the Yin to your Yang, the peanut butter to your chocolate, the Sonny to your Cher. And remember that your people are your lifeblood. They are critical to your forward movement and success. Take good care of your team from day one, and when you are the CEO of the next big thing, never forget that you got there because of them.

We touched briefly earlier on Seth Godin's concept of a tribe—a group around you who can both support you and give you constructive criticism and encouragement to help you achieve your best self, in business and in life. In the business world, a tribe includes your staff.

If you haven't yet discovered your unique brilliance zone, you must review **Super Power One** and pinpoint your skills and talents, using the Kolbe A Index and Stengthsfinder 2.0 assessments. You won't be able to find team members who complement you if you haven't discovered your unique brilliance zone and your business style and structure.

Once you know your strengths, you can then turn to finding staff whom compliment you, and again, the Kolbe is critical here. How you operate on a day-to-day or week-to-week basis, what you enjoy doing and what you really don't enjoy, will help you see where certain balls might get dropped. Do you hate administrative tasks? Your file room is going to be a disaster—hire an administrative assistant. Do you freeze on the phone because sales aren't your strong suit? Hire an enthusiastic sales or business development person to pick up the slack.

You may find yourself wanting to hire people like you, because you will immediately feel a strong connection—but that will only make your weak areas weaker. Look for people who can strengthen your business in the areas were you may lack.

BECOME A 3D Entrepreneur!

DELEGATE: This means off-loading the task or project to someone else, which could be a traditional W-2 team member, a virtual team member, or a vendor. When you delegate the task, describe what you want the end result to be and then empower your team member to accomplish the task the best way for them—don't try to dictate how they accomplish the task (provide it's legal, ethical, and in alignment with your company's value/culture).

DEFER: This is something that's a good – or even great idea – that worth exploring, just not right now. Too many entrepreneurs suffer from the "bright shiny object" syndrome and allow themselves to be distracted from their primary strategic focus when exposed to another intriguing idea or concept. Practice quickly examining ideas to see if they belong in the "deferral box" – as in good idea, but not now or the delete box.

DELETE: This is a task that really serves no purpose and is just a distraction. Sometimes it seems important, but really isn't. If you determine a task or project really isn't worthwhile, either now or in the future, it's time to hit the delete button and get rid of it. It's never ceases to amaze how many organizations of all sizes continue to perform outdated or even useless tasks because "that's the way we've always done it." Don't be afraid to ask "Why?" when confronted with a task that just doesn't make sense!

Delegation doesn't just extend to those you hire to help your business—it can extend into your personal life, as well. Maybe you hate grocery shopping, or cleaning the house, or running to the post office to mail your aunt's birthday present. These are time and energy drains that you can easily outsource—if you're worth $150 an hour, and you can pay a maid $15 an hour, why not outsource that part of your life, too? You'll save hours of time and reduce your stress level. Outsourcing these small tasks can allow you to live in that unique brilliance zone, ideally up to 70 or 80 percent of the time.

The 3 Biggest Lies We Tell Ourselves About Building a Team

LIE #1 – IT'S TOO EXPENSIVE:

This is a BIG lie and often the one that costs us the most money (for several reasons). Typically, we won't delegate or outsource things we find difficult or time-consuming because we think it will cost too much to do so. Here's an example of the erroneous "mental math" most of us engage in. Let's say you really don't like doing the monthly financials for your business and it takes you ten hours each month to complete the task, with lots of procrastinating and getting distracted. When someone suggests you hire a good bookkeeper or accountant to handle these chores, you recoil in horror and think 'No way…a good bookkeeper costs $75 an hour and it takes me 10 hours to do everything…so I'd rather keep my $750 and continue doing it myself!' This mental math is all wrong, and very likely to keep your business stuck.

Here's the truth: It takes you 10 hours to complete those tasks because you dislike doing them and aren't very good at it. A great bookkeeper who LOVES doing business financials would probably accomplish this task in 2–3 hours, only costing you $150–$225…not $750! But that's only part of the equation. The opportunity cost of spending one of your most valuable resources - time - on tasks your ill-suited for and don't like is enormous. What would happen if you re-directed those ten torturous hours a month towards sales, connecting with your top clients? How much additional revenue could you bring in over the course of month? Now multiple that by 12 and see what the annual impact of lost opportunity cost is for the year. For most businesses, it is way too expensive not to hire a team.

LIE #2 – IT TAKES TOO MUCH TIME TO TRAIN THEM:

This is another short-sighted lie that keeps many businesses stuck. If you don't build repeatable, scalable systems in your business that are run by someone other than you, you'll never build a business that you can monetize through an internal/external sale. Training and cross-training is a crucial part of enduring success for any organization. After all, what happens if your expert in a critical business function quits, goes to work for the competition, get's hit by a bus, is out with an extended illness, or has to care for a sick family member? We've seen businesses literally grind to a halt due to the loss of a single team member.

In addition, if you – as the owner – is the person with all the key institutional knowledge, what happens to the business if you get sick and can't work or have to cut back significantly? If you haven't taken the time to train others, this could be catastrophic for your business.

Think outside the box when it comes to training your team. Use audio and/or video recordings to document how you do certain tasks and then have those transcribed into an operations manual or archived in a video training library. Make sure you document every repetitive task and break down complex activities into digestible bits for easy consumption. Just a small amount of time invested in training (and cross-training) on key tasks will yield big dividends.

LIE #3 – IT'S EASIER TO DO IT MYSELF:

Business guru Michael E. Gerber admonishes business owners to work ON their business – not IN their business – in his classics *The E-Myth* and *The E-Myth Revisited*. He's exactly right! We already noted in Lie #2 above that not having repeatable and scalable systems in your business will greatly decrease the value of your business should you try to sell it in the future and the same is true if you simply try to handle all the key tasks yourself. If you're business can't survive and continue to make money if you're gone for 2 or more weeks, you're doing TOO much in the organization.

And this isn't only a problem tied to actually physically doing tasks. Some business owners don't empower their team members to make independent decisions…requiring all issues – small, medium, or large – to pass across their desk. This can be deadly to organizations for three reasons: (1) If you're not there, no key decisions are being made (2) if your team can't operate effectively without you, you'll probably never be able to spend more than a week away from the business without it falling apart and (3) your best team members will quickly become dis-satisfied with the lack of autonomy and eventually seek employment elsewhere. So ditch your perfectionist gene and loosen your grip on the reins a bit…you'll be surprised at what your team can do if you give them some leeway!

A critical component in building a successful collaborative relationship is making sure your venture is set up for success from a legal standpoint. First, you'll need a very clear legal agreement between you and your clients: one that sets out the scope of the work to be done and both party's limitations, as well as milestones for deliverable. Have a similar agreement for each Team Member, detailing expectations like hours worked and tasks completed. It's a good idea for clients to require clear communication monthly, especially on invoices and payment issues. Otherwise, you will have disputes or problems about finances down the road.

ALL SYSTEMS GO: Once you've been running the business for a while, it's important to delegate as much as possible (but see Super Power Four - Curiosity to understand when it is too soon to incur the cost of delegation). With delegation, you can set up systems and automate much more than you think.

For instance, create a detailed operations manual so that anyone can step in and run the business in a pinch if, for some reason, you are unable to. Do everything you can to avoid having anyone on your team reinvent the wheel. You don't want to pay someone twice for the same thinking or same work. Every time your team member does something new, have them write out the steps they took (including important website URLs, data or contact information) and put it in a new section of your operations manual. Require your team to update that weekly.

By doing this, you are starting to set up systems. Setting up these systems will give you flexibility and freedom to focus on what you are brilliant at doing. That isn't to say that you won't be bored or frustrated even with topics you're excited about, but focusing on your zone of genius is the best way to use your time when building a business.

This all sounds well and good, but even if you get the idea of Delegate, Defer and Delete down, you could still face high turn over or a less than enthused team. You could still have problems that don't get solved and you could end up treading water in your business. No, to get ahead in the new economy, you need to help your team. The best bosses in the world lead by inspiring and empowering their teams to excel and innovate. So how do you inspire a team to do that? What are the most important things to Team Members of most businesses? Do you know? The answer might surprise you.

But first, we want to tell you about a very interesting test conducted in the 1940s by a very smart scientist that is now called Duncker's Candle Problem ...

Duncker's Candle Problem:

Gestalt psychologist, Karl Duncker, created a cognitive performance test in the 1940s that he presented for his thesis on problem solving tasks at Clark University. In the test, the participant was told that they needed to figure out how to affix a lit candle on a wall (a cork board) in a way that would prevent wax from dripping onto the table below it. To accomplish this, the participant was given a book of matches and a box of thumbtacks. The participants were not given any help or instructions on how to accomplish this task successfully.

What the participants did not know is that the solution was to actually empty the box of thumbtacks, put the candle into that box and then use the thumbtacks to affix the box to the wall. After that, they should light the candle with the matches.

What was interesting, though, is that many of the people who attempted the test explored other creative, but less efficient, methods to achieve the goal. For example, some tried to tack the candle to the wall without using the thumbtack box. Others tried to melt some of the candle's wax and use it to stick the candle to the wall. Obviously, neither of those methods works. Very few tried to use the box in the "correct" way.

The outcome changed, however, if when the participant was given the task, the tacks were not IN the box but next to it. In that case, almost everyone discovered the best solution of using the candle to hold the box and the tacks to affix the box to the wall. That was because the answer was a lot more obvious.

It was apparently the fact that the box was already being used for the tacks that prevented most of the participants from using the box for any other purpose.

Since that time, this test has been done in many settings including MIT with some variations that are very important for this book. In those tests, some of the participants were offered cash prizes for completing the task quickly. There were told that the time it took them to solve the problem would determine the amount of cash they would win. The ones who could win a prize did better, right? Wrong. Amazingly, in that scenario, the ones who were offered prizes performed much worse than those who were not. The reasons given for this are based in the fact that having a prize on the line and being timed creates stress, which leads to "fight-or-flight" responses in the participants. Stress, then, effectively shut down the creative thinking and problem solving areas of the brain. Wow.

So how does this apply to us? It means that everything we have believed in our culture about how to motivate behavior is wrong. None of us are motivated by or perform better when under stress. And in an economy and time in history when innovation, creativity and problem-solving skills are vital to our position as an economic power, this information is revolutionary.

"EVERYTHING WE HAVE BELIEVED IN OUR CULTURE ABOUT HOW TO MOTIVATE BEHAVIOR IS WRONG"
– Daniel Pink

Let's take that one step further. Daniel Pink, best selling author and former speechwriter for Al Gore, has taken the Candle Problem and explained the ramifications for business owners. In his Ted talk, The Puzzle of Motivation, he explains what "social scientists know but most managers don't: Traditional rewards aren't always as effective as we think." He uses the Candle Problem as a springboard to outline what actually does motivate behavior. According to his research, "carrots and sticks" (promise of reward or threat of punishment) do not improve performance – they are detrimental to it. Especially when you need creative, outside of the box thinking (sorry – bad pun).

Daniel Pink says, "If you want people to perform better, you reward them, right? Bonuses, commissions, their own reality show. Incentivize them…But that's not happening here. You've got an incentive designed to sharpen thinking and accelerate creativity, and it does just the opposite. It dulls thinking and blocks creativity."

What does motivate people? According to Pink:

1. AUTONOMY: the urge to direct our own lives;

2. MASTERY: the desire to get better and better at something;

3. PURPOSE: the yearning to do what we do in the service of something larger than ourselves.

As Pink says, "These are the building blocks of an entirely new operating system for our businesses."

So what that really means it that in order to have an engaged and motivated staff, you must provide them not with carrots and sticks, but with the chance to have autonomy, mastery and purpose. This will not only keep them happy, but will produce their absolute best work. They will be more creative, will solve problems more easily, and will naturally innovate. It is the antidote to the Worker Bee issue we described in this book – that until now, our educational system created and rewarded Worker Bees. Trust us, you don't want Worker Bees. While there is definitely low level work required with any business, you want to seek out Team Members who are fully engaged and thinking critically and creatively at all times. It will make the execution of even the most base-level tasks that much better.

THE REALITY IS THAT WE HAVE TO RADICALLY CHANGE HOW WE ENGAGE AND TREAT OUR TEAM MEMBERS. This takes creativity on your part, because you will need to spend more time figuring out what makes your team members tick. What kind of autonomy can you give them? How can you help them achieve mastery over their expertise or workload? How can you help them find a sense of purpose? These are critical questions to ask, and you can't ask them if you left your humanity at the door, can you? In fact, we hope that you can answer how to achieve all three of those things for yourself first (if not, go back to Super Power One and do the work!). Then, roll up your sleeves and figure out how to discover the answer to each of these questions for everyone on your team.

PRIORITIZE: Need some additional help determining which business activities each of your team members should be focusing on and which ones to move off their plate and reassign? Please flip to the 3-Column Exercise we gave you on page 92–93 and have each team member complete the exercise. This 10 minute exercise will be enormously enlightening as to what each team member should be spending their time doing for your business.

PRACTICE WHAT YOU PREACH

LARRY BROUGHTON

broughtonHOTELS and BROUGHTONadvisory

How do you give your team members PURPOSE? We know of one CEO who does it brilliantly. Larry Broughton of broughtonHOTELS and Broughton Advisory Group.

Larry is an award-winning entrepreneur & CEO, best-selling author, keynote speaker and mentor, who spent eight years traveling the world with the US Army's elite Special Forces, commonly known as the Green Berets. During this time, he was awarded Outstanding Non-Commissioned Officer of his battalion and attained the rank of Staff Sergeant. Larry took his unique experience of serving on Special Forces A-Teams to the business arena. Now, he is Founder/CEO of broughtonHOTELS (www.broughtonHOTELS.com), a leader in the boutique hotel industry; and Co-Founder/CEO of Broughton Advisory Group (www.BROUGHTONadvisory.com), a strategic vision, elite team building, and transformational leadership organization with clients ranging from entrepreneurial start-ups to Turner Broadcasting and The Pentagon. He's received numerous awards for business performance, innovation and leadership; including Ernst & Young's prestigious Entrepreneur of the Year®, NaVOBA'S (National Veteran-Owned Business Association) Vetrepreneur® of the Year, Coastline Foundation's Visionary of the Year, while *Entrepreneur* Magazine included broughtonHOTELS in their Hot 500 List.

And despite his amazing record, he is very hands on and involved with this team on a daily basis. He also is a big believer in being of service. "No matter your circumstance, serve others. You'll find joy there, and it's the greatest vehicle to fulfillment in life," says Larry.

And he knows a thing or two about bringing his team together for a bigger cause. "On the first Friday of every month, everyone at broughtonHOTELS home office participates in our **PB&J First Fridays** event. During the event, we team up, make peanut butter and jelly sandwich sack lunches and donate all the food items to Share Our Selves (SOS), a nonprofit organization providing the highest quality comprehensive safety net services to the homeless and low-income populations of Orange County, California," explains Larry. They often partner with other companies to increase the impact of that event. Broughton has enlisted the help of vendors and clients (including TravelClick, Ralph's, Gilchrist & Soames, Sceptre Hospitality, Axis Purchasing, Standard Textile, and GCommerce) to provide more than 150 meals to SOS each month, and more than 4,500 meals to Southern Californians in need during the past twelve months.

broughtonHOTELS COO, Jim Sichta, expressed his gratitude to all who become involved with PB&J First Fridays. "The peanut butter and jelly challenge continues to grow each month, and with the continued support of our valued vendor partners & sponsors, we'll be able to continue supporting many more of those that desperately need help in our community. We all feel very blessed that we have this opportunity to make a difference."

We think it is a wonderful way to enable your team to find a sense of purpose in what they do. It is a great example of leadership in the new economy and Larry definitely qualifies as one of our New Super Heroes.

"At some point on your journey you'll find yourself questioning who you are and whether you've made the right choices. Sure, it helps at times to reflect and be critical of yourself and the choices you've made— this can sharpen your edge, create positive change, and foster new opportunities. But, before you get too critical, remember there's honor in strong and selfless leadership. Be sure not to think too much about how things could've been if you had made your choices differently. It's a destructive waste of time—and you can't go back and change what you did yesterday. Instead, look toward the future—take responsibility for your choices, and keep reminding yourself of the privilege it is to be a leader. Are you at peace with your leadership style?"–Larry Broughton.

_____

_____

_____

_____

_____

_____

_____

_____

_____

_____

_____

_____

_____

_____

_____

_____

_____

_____

_____

_____

_____

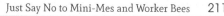

6

op·ti·mism, n.

ௐ W

1. A tendency to expect the best possible outcome or dwell on the most hopeful aspects of a situation; to see the best in all things;

2. A state of mind in which one always hopes or expects that something good will happen;

3. hopefulness; confidence;

4. *The Wonder Women Way:* Support is the thing you need, but optimism is what support gives you. Being with your tribe and strong mentors gives you the optimism you need to continue.

OPTIMISM

Finding Your Tribe and Mentors to Guide Your Success

The most successful people never go it alone.

You will need a team, mentors and a supportive and collaborative group of colleagues and friends. Think about it – the people you choose to spend time with, to allow into your world and your life have an enormous influence.

It has been proven time and time again. So you have to choose who you surround yourself with carefully. Choose people you admire, respect and want to be like. Select people who either share similar goals and aspirations, or those who believe in you so much that they will be there to support you and cheer you on as you go.

You become like the five people you spend the most time with. Choose carefully.
– Jim Rohn

3 Components to YOUR TRIBE!

We believe your tribe is ultimately comprised of three distinct, inter-related groups, including:

YOUR IDEAL CLIENTS/CUSTOMERS: These tribe members are the lifeblood of your business, since they will purchase your product/service. Designing your product/service to solve their biggest challenges, engaging them at an emotional level, providing outstanding service, and soliciting their feedback are great ways to engage this portion of your tribe.

YOUR COLLEAGUES/FELLOW ENTREPRENEURS: Successful entrepreneurs of today and tomorrow willing embrace collaborative and cooperative success. They connect with other like-minded entrepreneurs who are serving similar clientele and seek to provide complimentary – not competitive – products/services. They freely share resources and referrals, form strategic alliances and joint ventures, and actively cheer each other on to greater heights. They selflessly serve each other and believe they win when others win too.

YOUR MENTORS/COACHES: These seasoned entrepreneurs and experts have already walked the path ahead of you and can save you ENORMOUS amounts of time, frustration, and money. They are so important that the second half of this chapter discusses them in more detail.

We all need a tribe of our own that gets us and what we are trying to do in our time on this earth. Often, that tribe is not going to be made up of the people in your family or your closest friends. You can adore them, but chances are that they don't get you or what you are doing. In fact, they might even be baffled, frustrated or downright angry about your chosen path. That kind of energy can be debilitating to an entrepreneur, so make sure you balance that out with the support, encouragement and inspiration of other entrepreneurs who understand you.

This is not a new concept. Think of the quote from the movie *Gladiator*. During a scene when Russell Crowe's character and his fellow gladiators – cast as the "barbarian horde" – are about to fight for their lives against enormous odds in the Roman Colosseum, Crowe's character shouts to them, **"If we stay together, we will survive!"** Simple, profound, and absolutely true.

Even the big corporations have tribes. They are called boards of directors. The idea of using the collective experiences and wisdom of the group to better the organization. Who else uses a tribe? The President. It is called his Cabinet. It is the same concept and there hasn't been a single president in modern U.S. history that attempted to execute his presidency without his "tribe" counseling him on a daily basis. You may not be fighting terrorists or the Roman Legionnaires, but you are fighting a battle every day – a battle for authenticity, for a business on your own terms, for financial independence and for credibility and success in your small (or large) corner of the world. It would be unwise to go it alone.

IDENTIFYING YOUR IDEAL CLIENTS

Effectively engaging your tribe requires authenticity, transparency, and commitment. Bland copy, "me too" websites, and uninteresting offers simply won't keep people engaged today. Ultimately, people want to do business with other people that they know, like, and trust and the only way to develop your KLT (know, like, trust) Factor is by sharing who you are, what you believe (and why), and what you stand for.

Own it. Be unapologetic about it. Don't compromise it.

Now this means that you'll turn some people off and they won't want to do business with you. That's a good thing! Trying to be all things to all people is a recipe for disaster and just because a prospect can fog up a mirror and pay your fees doesn't mean you should work with them. Smart entrepreneurs – especially in the service arena – understand that it's critical to interview the clients just as much as they are interviewing you. If your gut tells you a prospect isn't a good fit, listen to the warning bells and let them pass. The wrong client can literally suck the life out of you and make your entrepreneurial life a living hell.

TRAIN YOUR CLIENTS: Your clients will treat you however you TRAIN them to treat you. So if you train your clients that it's okay to call you 24 hours a day, 7 days a week, 365 days a year – don't complain when they call you on your anniversary, your vacation, or your kid's birthday. On the other hand, if you set reasonable boundaries and manage expectations on access and availability, you can build a business that's actually compatible with your life.

IDENTIFYING YOUR IDEAL COLLEAGUES

Get clear on what you offer and who you are in competition with. Although the point of collaborative capitalism is not maintaining the age-old competitive mindset that has so hindered ethical business practices, you still need to be aware of businesses with similar offerings. If your dream is to open a cupcake shop, but there's already a popular bakery in your small town of six hundred people, yours probably won't do well—so the focus is not on competition, per se, but on a common sense analysis of whether there's room for you in the market. Instead of focusing on a rigid conception of what you want, consider both what the market is looking for and how you can best meet that need.

Researching which businesses provide a service or product that complements yours is also key. Combined, you and another business can offer something more valuable together than either of you could alone, strengthening your position in the market and building a loyal and thriving client base. The secret to approaching another business with an offer to combine products or services is to consider what you have to offer them—what will benefit them, not you. Of course, you'll want it to benefit you, too, but if you pitch it that way your potential partner will immediately be turned off from the proposal. People are more willing to take a favor than give one. So, offer something of value to them, something that benefits their clients, prospects, or bottom line. Open your mind to how the relationship can be win-win. Remember, other entrepreneurs are just as busy as you are—you'll have to be convincing and succinct to get their attention and, eventually, their partnership.

INSIDER TIP

If you don't approach networking correctly, you'll anger potential contacts instead of winning them to your side. Don't immediately start pitching your business or asking for favors—chat normally and forge a personal connection before you get down to the nitty-gritty contours of office talk. Importantly, don't add them to your email list just because they friended you on Facebook or gave you a business card—this is a violation of the Federal Can Spam Act, which carries monetary penalties. Instead, ask them for permission first—if they give you a business card, ask right then and then mark the card with a "Y" or "N" and file it in your records.

No one—from presidents and tycoons of business to prima ballerinas and award-winning photographers—made it to the top without help from others who had already been there and could guide them on their way.

Consider some of the benefits of a mentor:

- serves as an impartial sounding board for your ideas

- has already made the mistakes so you don't have to

- provides support and encouragement or, alternatively, the harsh reality.

There's an archetype in American culture of the entrepreneur who pulled him- or herself up by her bootstraps and made it all on his or her own. That's a blatant fallacy. It's critical to align yourself with other people who can help you on your path to success rather than deter you from it or send you down dead ends.

As mentioned before, but it bears repeating, consider the most powerful companies and our country's most powerful man, the President. They all have mentors. Companies have a board of directors who oversee the firm's operations and decision-making, following a certain set of values and bylaws. They give guidance on the day-to-day operations of the business. The President has a Cabinet, people he has hand-selected from a variety of expertise and backgrounds, who are available to hash out issues with. (You could call that his tribe.) Not everyone in your life will be supportive and encouraging of your new dream—in fact, many might not be. As we've discussed in previous chapters, America is deeply invested in its time-honored way of doing business: only one winner, certain hours in an office, particular definitions of what it means to succeed.

And people who don't understand may often try to question your decisions. Take note that questioning your decisions in itself is not negative—you can always benefit from constructive criticism. But someone who is tearing you down is toxic, and you must limit your exposure to toxic people or risk getting derailed or disheartened. In fact, that's the first reason you need the advice and support of a mentor.

REASON NO. 1 TO FIND A MENTOR: SUPPORT IN THE FACE OF THE NAYSAYERS

Friends, family, and business colleagues in your life may have many reasons for discouraging your dreams of entrepreneurship—they may be afraid that you'll go under financially and not be able to support your family, they may not want you to feel the pain of failing, or they may even just be jealous that they're not brave enough to step outside of the corporate box themselves. Regardless of the reason, their criticism can be disheartening and even, in the case of spouses or parents, heartbreaking. You may struggle with feelings of doubt and sadness or anger that they don't believe in you.

That's where engaging the services of a mentor becomes vitally important. But before we go on with this topic, note one thing: unless you're already well-connected, you're probably not going to find a mentor for free. You can't just walk up to Oprah or Sir Richard Branson and ask for their guidance—they're busy and they don't have time. This may at first seem odd to you, but remember that to you, time is money—and it's the same for other people.

Paying a mentor doesn't mean you're getting any less of a service or inferior advice. On the contrary, it means your mentor is specially invested in your success. When money is tight, however, a mentor can seem like an absurd expense—if you look at is as an expense. Instead, recast the idea of a mentor in your mind as an investment in your most valuable asset: you. **The more you can bring to your business, the more successful that business will be—and a mentor can accelerate your growth.**

Furthermore, the guidance of a mentor in your life may quiet some of the toxic people around you. Mentors are people who have had great success in their field and know the ins and outs of the business—they command respect. Being connected to such a person will likely make your friends and family have a little more respect for your ideas, as well. If someone who is successful believes in you, then your idea just might be something with promise.

If the toxic person is extraneous (say, your old officemate who you really only talk to on the train), then cut them out—their negative energy is poisoning you. If the toxic person is a loved one, then try to first explain your business concept and share your passion with them before telling them that you appreciate their support but don't necessarily need their advice—after all, you're paying someone for that.

Finally, if you are getting negative feedback from these toxic people, don't judge your business or prospects by others' words. Instead, judge it by the data that you've gathered—compare it to your personal mission statement, your understanding of your target market, sales numbers, etc. That will reveal your true potential for success.

Toxic people may also be eager to jump on any mistakes you make as an indicator of your destiny to fail, which leads to the second reason a mentor is vital to finding and staying in your unique brilliance zone.

"DON'T LET SOMEONE WHO GAVE UP ON THEIR DREAMS TALK YOU OUT OF YOURS." – Unknown

REASON NO. 2 TO FIND A MENTOR: AVOIDING MISTAKES

There are no new mistakes in business—no matter how different you think your situation is, we promise it's already been addressed and solved by another entrepreneur. Unfortunately, mistakes can cost you money, time, reputation, or even your business. So why make them in the first place? A mentor in your field can show you the warning signs and which pitfalls to avoid, or even areas you would never of thought of that could be a minefield (non-disclosure agreements, anyone?).

The words of advice from a mentor can result in great leaps in income, personal growth, and satisfaction that might have taken you years on your own. When you feel overwhelmed by a situation or just too close to it to see it clearly, a mentor can give you a new perspective. If you're chasing the wrong client or investing in a business model that doesn't suit your personality and work habits, a mentor can guide you in a new direction. Some of our most successful entrepreneurs today—including many of those mentioned in this book—have had and tout the benefits of a mentor.

Don't try to figure everything out on your own. Instead, spend time looking for people who can serve as resources—ask for referrals, recommendations, and guidance. Get every shred of information about the business you're in, and avoid trying to reinvent the wheel. Since there are no new mistakes or challenges in business, why not draw from someone else's wealth of knowledge? Otherwise it's an expensive lesson to learn once you factor in leasing an office, buying furniture, and hiring a secretary all before you have a paying client. Maybe your business doesn't even require an office—and a mentor would have told you that! Mentors can also connect you with manufacturers, press/media and influential people in your industry.

AVOID THE IAKT SYNDROME

The four most dangerous letters to an entrepreneur are IAKT – which stands for "I already know that..."

There's a huge difference between knowledge and action and just because you may know something intellectually, you may not be applying it (or applying it effectively). Never tell a mentor that you already know something. Even if you think you have something under control, listen to and consider their advice; be open to new ways of doing something and actively engage in a discussion with them about the possibilities. If you're introduced to something you truly already know and are implementing, be gracious and respond with "Great point... thanks for the reminder!

However, there is one mistake you can make with a mentor—hiring one who either doesn't have enough experience or who doesn't have enough expertise in your field. Someone with twenty years' experience as a business coach sounds great—but if they've been coaching businesses wholly different from yours, they may not understand enough about your particular industry to be an effective counselor. If they've never grown a business themselves, they might not have enough experience to guide you in many of the substantive aspects of business development. So, make sure they have experience and expertise—with technology what it is, it's easy to get a logo, business cards, and a website proclaiming that you're a business coach. There are no entry barriers or licensing requirements, so it's basically open season out there. Unfortunately, many so-called "business gurus" don't actually have much experience running real businesses – managing teams with P&L responsibility. The only real experience they have is running a coaching business. Make sure that you're learning from someone who's been there, done that in your industry and is still doing it.

Two benefits that you should and can derive from a productive mentor relationship are income and growth, which are achieved through a complex interplay of factors, not the least of which are effective networking and hard work.

Mentors can bring more to the table than just guidance—they can also provide a network of introductions. This network is something you should carefully consider before proceeding into the relationship—if the mentor can only introduce you to other new entrepreneurs who are struggling with their businesses as well, you might find daily support but you won't find the advice and introductions you need. The mentor should be able to connect you with business owners who have already become successful and who can help you as you enter that higher plane.

Also look at your mentor's other clients—are they on a similar journey, practicing the tenets of the conscious business revolution, or are they still stuck in the old, masculine mindset of succeeding in business under a "winning at all costs" manifesto? If you're dedicated to the Wonder Women business revolution,

THE RIGHT FIT: Do your research on a potential mentor, and get recommendations and referrals if possible. If someone doesn't feel like a right fit, then don't proceed into the relationship—and don't find someone to just be your "yes man" (a legitimate mentor will never fill that role). Look beyond testimonials and ask clients to tell you the good and the bad. After you've done that work and forged a partnership with someone, then it's time to start working that connection for the benefit of yourself and your business.

a mentor who is pushing you toward cutthroat business practices is not the best fit—and since mentors are expensive, you want the best, most beneficial relationship possible.

A good rule of thumb is to never spend more than 10 percent of your personal income on mentoring services. This will also spur you to look for more successful mentors as you uplevel—the more successful you are, the higher level mentor you will need and the more you will be able to spend on one. While it can be hard to let go of a mentor who has nurtured and guided you, there will always be a time to move on. An authentic, sincere mentor will recognize this. Beware of the mentor who tries to hold you back and doesn't encourage you to move forward. They are likely more invested in their own bank account than in your success.

The best method of mentoring will also change as you continue along your entrepreneurial journey. In the early stages of your progress, group coaching is ideal—you will receive a lot of content, probably more than you can implement from month to month. You'll also find centers of support and collaboration in other group members. Eventually, though, the generalized advice you receive in group sessions won't be enough to keep you moving. You'll need one-on-one mentoring to receive answers to specific questions that are completely centric to your situation and your business. With one-on-one mentoring, you can receive phone conferences or even VIP days, where you spend an entire day with your coach, strategizing and mapping out the nuts and bolts of certain items of your business.

Another vital way to get the most out of the relationship, and one many overlook, is to take full responsibility for your own work and progress. The mentor is not there to do the work for you—only to give guidance and feedback. The company lives or dies with your effort, not the mentor's. It's easy to jump to placing blame on a mentor if things aren't going well, but often times you just need to roll up your sleeves. The program is not the key to success—you are.

Finally, make sure that your mentor thoroughly understands not only how you tick (based on Kolbe or Strengthsfinder assessments that we discussed earlier in the book) but also what you want. Not everyone wants to build an empire, and not everyone wants to stay small. An effective mentor tailors their coaching to your end goals, not their personal conception of success. An effective mentor is also honest about the hardships of the path to success. You need to get behind the curtain and receive full disclosure about how long it took that mentor to get where they are, how things operate, and what kinds of money are required for certain levels of success.

But success stories don't happen overnight, so a coach who makes promises without talking about reality is probably not authentic. Anyone who touts only one way to corner the business market is not a viable candidate for a mentoring relationship, because no mentor has the magic bullet to success. Rather, a mentor should analyze your strengths and use those to offset your shortcomings, shaping a business plan and strategy that is unique to you.

A mentor can encourage your great ideas and red-flag the less-than-promising ones; they can help you with marketing, streamlining systems, cutting expenses, and maximizing revenue. They can give you advice on team management and support you in the face of toxic people. In short, a mentor can set you up for success, and the importance of this relationship can't be emphasized enough. It's an invaluable investment in yourself and your business' potential.

Meet the New
SUPER HEROES!

TARYN ROSE, Taryn Rose Shoes

In 1998, Taryn Rose changed the footwear industry forever with her line of luxury shoes that were fashionable and functional. Her brand has become one of the most successful and highly coveted brands in footwear. What started in her garage grew to a 40 million dollar business with boutiques all over the country. She ultimately sold the company for a healthy profit, right before the onset of the Great Recession.

Taryn Rose has been recognized for her numerous honors and has been featured on television, and in newspapers and magazines including *Oprah, CNN, Today Show, New York Times, People* magazine, *Entrepreneur, In Style, Elle, Lucky, O* magazine, *British Vogue, Town & Country* and countless more. She also gives back by supporting organizations and projects such as Breast Cancer Research Center in New York, Memorial Sloan Kettering Cancer Center, Children's Hospital Los Angeles, AIDS Project Los Angeles, Clothes Off Our Back, Lynne Cohen Foundation and Step Up Women's Network.

But her story is far from a fairytale, and the path to success wasn't smooth or easy. Taryn was raised in a very conservative Vietnamese family that expected her to be a doctor, just like her father was. And the pressure to please her family was strong. They escaped from Vietnam for the US when Taryn was 8. Born in Ho Chi Minh City, Vietnam in 1967, she narrowly escaped with her family three days before the fall of Saigon. The family left everything they owned, boarded a plane amidst machine guns and artillery fire, and started a new life in the States.

After graduating from college, she chose to attend USC's Medical School to study orthopedic surgery. Taryn wanted to follow in her Pathologist father's footsteps of medicine. By doing so, she would keep her family happy (i.e. avoid family drama). She also had a desire to "work with healthy people and get them back to their best."

But her medical career did not go as it "should" have gone.

A lover of great shoes, she was known for wearing 3-inch Prada heels in surgery. But as an orthopedic surgeon, she got the chance to see the serious foot problems that existing fashion footwear caused. So early in her residency, she decided to create a line of shoes that were both chic but also comfortable, and that took anatomy and foot biomechanics into account.

Fear of failure was something she struggled with as she began to launch the company. "I could hear my friends and family saying, 'Why did you leave a secure job?' If I failed, would I be okay facing them? And I thought, So what? I can go back to do a fellowship. I started to accept that it would be okay to say, 'I failed, but I tried.' Once I was comfortable with that scenario, the fear dissolved. I realized that I feared regret more than failure...I'd rather live with failure than regret...Failure you can deal with, regret you can't change, because it's too late."

It is Taryn's courage and determination against great pressure and odds that lands her on our list of the New Super Heroes.

☐ **Before you hire a mentor or business coach, ask her the following questions:**

> 1) Who have you coached and in what industry?
>
> 2) Have you coached in my industry?
>
> 3) What is your education, training, experience and track record when coaching businesses like mine?
>
> 4) What are you really good at that your clients benefit from?
>
> 5) What kinds of issues did your clients in my industry face, and how did you help them? What measurable results did they have?
>
> 6) What is your area of expertise or zone of genius?
>
> 7) How long do clients stay with you? Is there an ideal amount of time a client should work with you to see ideal results?
>
> 8) How soon is it realistic to begin seeing results in my business (based on your other clients' experiences)?
>
> 9) What is your Kolbe score and Strengthfinders score?
>
> 10) Please provide me with references from current and past clients.

☐ **In addition, be very clear about your needs. After reading this book, you should have a good idea what you need the most help with. Make sure that the coach or mentor you work with specializes in the areas you need.**

Here are some ideas for quick reference:

- Time Management

- Financial Management

- Team Building and Management

- Launching a company

- Growing a company

- Operations and Systems

- Growing your email list and internet-based marketing

- Mindset

- Leadership

- Sales

- Marketing

- PR and media

- Speaking

- Writing and publishing a book

☐ Set goals for your work with this coach. Where do you want to be when the work with this coach is done? Be as specific as you can. Write it down and keep it handy so you can look at it regularly and make sure you are on track. Tell your coach your specific goals so she can help support you in getting there.

Addressing these issues will create appropriate expectations for the relationship, and will give you measurable milestones to track to determine if the relationship is a success.

But remember, any growth or progress you make is up to YOU. Your coach is a resource, but no one can implement what you learn but you. If you aren't getting what you hoped out of the relationship, be very careful about trying to blame your coach or mentor. First ask yourself what you could be doing (or not doing) to prevent your forward movement.

NOTES

7

cour·age, n.

⸺ ⱳ**W** ⸺

1. The state or quality of mind or spirit that enables one to face danger, fear, or vicissitudes with self-possession, confidence, and resolution; bravery;

2. The mental or moral strength to venture, persevere, and withstand danger, fear, or difficulty;

3. *The Wonder Women Way:* You can persist without courage and keep hitting a brick wall. You need courage to "do the thing you think you cannot do." – Eleanor Roosevelt.

COURAGE

Fall Down Seven Times.
Get Up Eight.

There are those who would lead you to believe that if you do entrepreneurship right, you will easily make six-figures in sixty days (or something like that). Or, others will tell you that you will quickly get funded and be able to retire at the age of 30.

Those of us who are real entrepreneurs – the ones who have lasted through hardship, failure and fear – will tell you the truth: **Entrepreneurship is not for the faint of heart.** It is hard. It is scary. It is a nail biter in every sense of the word. It will test you to your breaking point and cost you blood, sweat and tears.

At first glance it may appear too hard. Look again. Always look again.

– Mary Anne Rodmacher

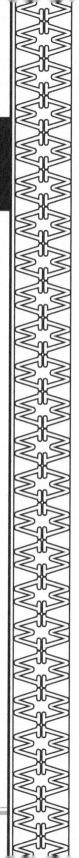

Remember, most "overnight successes" are 10–15 years in the making. Some say entrepreneurship is the best personal development tool out there – way better than therapy! It certainly will stretch you to your limits.

{ DO IT ANYWAY }

If you have stuck with us this far, then here is what you know:

- You now know yourself well – you know what makes you tick, what you are passionate about, what you are really good at, and what your personal mission statement is.

- You know what you want your company to accomplish.

- You also know how to build a world-class team who will support you in your life's mission, and you know how to keep them motivated and happy.

- You know how to protect your hard work, and you are no longer afraid to look your business finances in the eye.

So you are ready. Ready to start, ready to move forward, ready to reboot. At moments like this, it is easy to move ahead and do what needs to be done. When you have a new fire in your belly and a clear path ahead, nothing can stop you. It is the best feeling in the world.

But you know that won't last, right? We wish it would – goodness knows we have both spent sleepless nights wishing for that passion, clarity and optimism to return. Well you know what? It will. But it will fade again too. That is life. Just like a great relationship or marriage, the emotional fun of it will come and go. But what makes it really fulfilling and a true success story is what happens when it isn't necessarily fun. **It is the sticking with it that will help you become a better CEO, better manager, better boss, better person.**

So...the sooner you accept the fact that it is going to be hard, the better. Not because we want to kill your enthusiasm. We want the fan the flame of your excitement, not douse it. But we also want you to go into this (or continue with it) with your eyes wide open. Just like it is critical to look your money in the eye, it is also critical to look into the future with realism and knowledge. As it has been said for generations, "knowledge is power." We want you to know what lies ahead so you aren't broadsided or discouraged by it. We also want you to know that when you do hit that rough patch, you are not alone. Any real business owner has been there. And sometimes, the rough patches can last a long time. If you were in business before the markets crashed in 2008, then you know how interminable it can feel when the rough patch persists. But it always...always... ends. If you stick with it.

Of course, being a survivor requires not just blind optimism or persistence, although both can help a lot (we are only joking about the blind part). But being a survivor requires having a plan in case of emergencies.

Think of the safety procedure announcements that happen on a plane every time you fly. They repeat that announcement every flight because they want you to be prepared. They aren't telling you how to prepare for the worst-case scenario because they want you to run screaming off the plane. They want you to take the ride. Well...so do we. And our hope is that this book has given you the roadmap to help you navigate through anything – fat or lean times. We also hope that you will come back and read and re-read what we have written, because it is not just for the here and now, but it is a "safety procedures" manual in the event of emergency. And unlike on a plane, where the odds are you will never need to use the safety procedures they outline, in this case, you will most definitely need the guidance we have provided in this book. And you will want to revisit the notes you have kept as you read each chapter. They will help you stay on course, much like a lighthouse helps a ship navigate through the dense fog.

Then, get out there and find your tribe and your mentors. There is nothing more difficult than weathering a storm alone and isolated. Find your support network now, so that when the storm hits, you will be safely nested in your community and ready for it. As the Boy Scouts say, "Be Prepared."

Meet the New
SUPER HEROES!

KEEP KNOCK, KNOCK, KNOCKING

SARA BLAKELY – Founder of innovative undergarment company Spanx (over $250 million in annual revenues) and world's youngest self-made billionaire.

This former Walt Disney World ride greeter and door-to-door office machine salesperson turned a frustrating clothing challenge for women – the elimination of unsightly panty lines – into a powerhouse garment company in just a few years. Gambling her entire life savings ($5,000) and operating from her Atlanta apartment, she spent two years researching and developing just the right material for her product.

Design in hand, she approached mill after mill in North Carolina to find a manufacturing facility to perfect her prototype and produce the product. Undaunted by numerous "No" responses, she kept at it until she got a yes. She then broke every accepted convention in undergarment packaging, rejecting the traditional boring appearance and going for something bold and eye-catching.

With no money for marketing or advertising, she embarked on a guerilla marketing and sales campaign which included pulling the buyer at Neiman Marcus into the dressing room to personally demonstrate the before-and-after results of Spanx, enlisting friends and family members to go to stores carrying the product and buy them up, and crisscrossing the country doing working directly with the sales floor associates and talking to shoppers.

Her belief in her product, relentless personal marketing, and determination to keep asking until she got a "Yes" resulted in Spanx taking off in record time, achieving $4 million in sales in the first year and $10 million in the second. Media mogul Oprah Winfrey named Spanx her favorite product of the year in 2000 and in 2001, Sara landed a gig with QVC.

Appearances on several entrepreneur-themed TV shows followed, along with the continued rapid growth of Spanx. In 2006, she formed the Sara Blakely Foundation to promote entrepreneurial training/education for women and donated $1 million to Oprah Winfrey's Leadership Academy. More recently, she joined fellow billionaires Warren Buffet and Bill Gates Giving Pledge, making the commitment to donate at least half her wealth to charity.

Find out more about her incredible story at **www.spanx.com.**

"SUCCESS IS NOT FINAL, FAILURE IS NOT FATAL: IT IS THE COURAGE TO CONTINUE THAT COUNTS. NEVER, NEVER, NEVER, NEVER GIVE UP." – WINSTON CHURCHILL

_____

_____

_____

_____

_____

_____

_____

_____

_____

_____

_____

_____

_____

_____

_____

_____

_____

_____

_____

_____

_____

_____

_____

_____

YOU DON'T NEED TO SEE THE ENTIRE STAIRCASE. JUST START CLIMBING.

– Martin Luther King Jr.

CONCLUSION

Hopefully this book has challenged you to reconsider how America does business. If you picked *Wonder Women* up off the shelf, you were probably already struggling with the current cutthroat mentality. Perhaps you were looking for an escape from corporate America, seeking guidance on how to improve your business, or wondering how to create a new business that positively impacts not only your own life, but that of your family, friends, and community.

More and more entrepreneurs are sensing this change, but not all are ready to embrace it. We urge you to take the lessons from this book and apply them to your own business and life. We invite you to come to our website and connect with us. Do you think our position is genius, or complete bunk? Are you facing a business road block or dealing with a toxic relationship? Have you had success implementing the steps we have given about how to launch a business and save the world? Let us know! We are anxious to hear from you and will be sharing success stories on our website every month!

And if what we're sharing here is impactful or enlightening, pass the information along to other women in business and entrepreneurs who can benefit from it—those who are searching for something more and open to a new way of doing business. Use the resources and tools on our website and check back in frequently for new advice and support.

It's time to don our capes and hone our superpowers! Let's fly!!

— Jessica Eaves Mathews & Phil Dyer

We hope you've enjoyed reading Wonder Women as much as we enjoyed putting it together and we welcome the opportunity to stay connected with you. After all, we believe that collaborative and cooperative business ventures are the wave of the future!

You can connect with us and keep up with latest developments in collaborative entrepreneurial success at **www.wonderwomenbook.com**

We are available to support individual business owners as well as organizations through:

o Keynote presentations for conferences & organizations

o Workshop facilitation for conferences & organizations

o Strategic offsite facilitation for organizations & executive teams

o Strategic mentoring for CEOs, entrepreneurs, small business owners & senior executives

o Director/Advisory Board positions for select organizations

Please don't hesitate to contact us if we can be of assistance.

You can also connect directly with us on LinkedIn at:

Jessica: www.linkedin.com/in/jessicaeavesmathews

Phil: www.linkedin.com/in/phillipdyer

JESSICA EAVES MATHEWS is America's Advocate for Women in Business™, an award-winning entrepreneur and intellectual property and business lawyer, published author and speaker, and leading authority on helping women entrepreneurs and women business owners step into their power and create a brilliant business and a brilliant life on their own terms. She has been featured on MSNBC, Oprah, Forbes.com, NBC, Oxygen, Allure Magazine and is the Silver Stevie award winner for Female Entrepreneur of the Year 2012. For more about Jessica, visit www.jessicaeavesmathews.com

Jessica has spent her legal career representing all types of businesses from solopreneurs to Fortune 500 companies. Before launching her own firm, she was the head of litigation and compliance for Paul Allen, the co-founder of Microsoft. Jessica is the founder of Leverage Legal Group®, the premier, global intellectual property and business law firm for the new economy. Jessica's team of exceptional, experienced attorneys provide world-class, flat fee legal services, virtual general and outside counsel, and in-sourced legal services. The firm's award-winning, entry-level program, Leverage-a-Lawyer®, provides budget-friendly, flat-fee legal services, information and education for first-time business owners or startups, who don't yet have the budget for full-blown legal counsel. Visit www.leveragelegalgroup.com for more information about the firm.

Jessica has continued to get experience "on the other side of the conference table" as Founder and CEO of Grace & Game®, the only luxury American lifestyle brand for both golf and for the sophisticated, feminine, modern women. Grace & Game designs are made in the USA with sustainable fabrics and are designed to perform beautifully both on and off the course. Look for Grace & Game online at www.graceandgame.com. She is also Founder and CEO of Untoxicating Beauty®, a new subscription beauty experience for women who care as much about what goes into their bodies as what they put on them. www.untoxicatingbeauty.com

She is also an adjunct professor at University of New Mexico Law School, co-founder and Chief Legal Officer for The Virtual Accelerator™, a business accelerator for startups, and is the co-founder of Hautepreneurs™, a new networking organization for women entrepreneurs based in Albuquerque, New Mexico.

PHIL DYER is an award-winning serial entrepreneur, best-selling author, writer and speaker. He is the Founder/CEO of Dyer Financial Advisory, LLC; a boutique fee-only financial planning/wealth management firm and Co-Founder/Chief Visionary of Broughton Advisory Group; a strategic planning, leadership development, and training company.

Phil is a graduate of the United States Military Academy at West Point and former Army Captain who now applies the leadership lessons learned in the service to today's dynamic business battlefield.

Since serving on active duty, Phil has achieved success in corporate, non-profit, and small business pursuits. Past areas of focus include medical sales for a Fortune 50 company, serving as the National Financial Educator for the Military Officers Association of America (MOAA) and numerous entrepreneurial ventures. Phil recently received the MVC (Most Valuable Contributor) Award from 300 small business peers for his innovations in marketing, business growth, and building virtual teams.

Over the past 17 years, Phil has counseled hundreds of entrepreneurs and thousands of transitioning military service members on financial, tax and business success strategies. He has given over 775 speeches worldwide on a variety of financial/business topics and has shared the stage with some of today's most innovative business thought leaders. Phil is a key driver in the rapidly growing military veteran entrepreneur movement and actively partners with leading organizations such as the Institute for Veterans and Military Families (IVMF) to train, coach, and mentor hundreds of current and aspiring "vetrepreneurs" each year.

A prolific writer, Phil has over 100 business/financial by-lines in major magazines and is frequently quoted in publications such as The Wall Street Journal, Money, Kiplinger's Personal Finance, Men's Health and many others. He is the co-author of including VICTORY: 7 Entrepreneur Success Strategies for Veterans (with Larry Broughton) and has received several APEX Awards for Publication Excellence. A strong believer in continual personal and professional development, Phil holds numerous professional designations, including: Certified Financial Planner, Registered Life Planner and Certified Co-Active Professional Coach.

A tireless advocate for collaborative and cooperative business ventures, Phil partners frequently with other forward-thinking entrepreneurs on innovative business ventures. He currently resides in Maryland horse country with his family.

CPSIA information can be obtained at www.ICGtesting.com
Printed in the USA
LVOW01s0213171015

458101LV00003B/4/P